SPIRITUAL STAMINA

—Stuart Briscoe—
SPIRITUAL STAMINA

Biblical Workouts for a Lasting Faith

MULTNOMAH

Portland, Oregon 97266

Cover design by Bruce DeRoos
Edited by Steve Halliday

SPIRITUAL STAMINA
©1988 by Multnomah Press
Portland, Oregon 97266

Printed in the United States of America

Library of Congress Cataloging-in-Publication Data

Briscoe, D. Stuart.
  Spiritual stamina / D. Stuart Briscoe.
    p. cm.
  Includes index.
  ISBN 0-88070-224-9: $10.95
    1. Bible. N.T. Colossians—study.   2. Spiritual life—Biblical
teaching.   I. Title.
BS2715.5B75 1988
227'.706—dc19   88-19097
                                                              CIP

Special thanks to Steve Halliday,
a gracious and gifted editor.

Contents

IV
Christian Ministries: Assisting Team Members

How Can I Get Involved?

V
Christian Warnings: Staying on Track

What Are Wolves Doing Here?

Introduction

The advertiser knew his craft. Early morning light streamed through the windows of a health club. Varied patterns of light danced on gleaming weights and rowing machines and Nautilus equipment and various other instruments of self-inflicted torture.

Into this scene walked a man in street clothes. He began to talk of all the benefits of working out and getting in good shape. And then, to my surprise, he held up a copy of the *New York Times*.

"Some of you may not be able to lift this," he said, pointing to the weights, "but you can lift this"—holding up the newspaper.

His point was simple and well taken. Many folks are interested in growing physically, in bulking up, in working out. That's great! But what about working out mentally? Who wants to be big in brawn but bare in brain? People need to do something to develop their intellectual grasp of the world around them.

Notice the line the salesman took. Starting with what people were interested in, he worked to the thing they were less interested in. He led them from a greater interest— physical wellness—to a lesser one—intellectual wellness.

Let me borrow from that advertisement. Some of you are lifting weights, jogging, dieting. You are vitally interested in conditioning your bodies and being physically fit. God bless you, so you should! I would encourage you to lift weights, and to lift the newspaper as well, to keep in touch with your body and in tune with your world.

But I want to go a step further. You need to be lifting your Bible as well.

If you really want to get in shape, make sure you're not only growing physically and intellectually, but spiritually.

That's what this book is all about. It's written for those who want to begin "spiritual weight training."

Have you just begun on the Christian journey and are unsure about what to do next? Then join me for some biblical workouts.

Or have you been a believer for a long time, become dissatisfied with your spiritual conditioning, and have decided it's time to get into shape? You are welcome as well.

We'll focus on highlights from Paul's epistle to the Colossians, a powerful little book for "people on the grow." We'll select a few key passages, arrange them by theme, and go from there.

Colossians is an ideal book for those who want to begin getting into shape spiritually. It contains one of the most solid, profound, condensed statements concerning the Lord Jesus Christ to be found anywhere in Scripture. Paul lays a solid theology in the book's first two chapters, then carefully applies that theology in the last two chapters.

Whenever you look into Scripture, you'll find things to believe and corresponding ways to behave. Never forget that for Christians, *believing* and *behaving* go hand in hand.

Some people want to believe in such a way that it doesn't affect their behavior. They like you to keep it theological, theoretical; they don't want it getting practical. That way they can keep their religion locked up for a convenient hour or so on a Sunday morning without having it intrude into the rest of their week.

Others say, "Don't bother me with theology; just give me something to help. Boy, I've had a terrible week. I've had to create, I've had to work, I've really been putting out all week. Don't make me think! I mean, religion is supposed to let you switch off your mind. Just give me something practical."

Paul says, "No, no, no! I'm not interested in quick fixes that won't last. I want you to understand that underlying the practical solutions to problems are profound theological principles."

This is one of the things that makes Paul so tremendously helpful. He gives us a theological base and on that base builds a practical application. He gives theological insight, then shows how that truth works out practically in everyday life.

He follows that pattern throughout Colossians. First, he states a certain truth. Then he applies that truth, and finally he requires some action of obedience based on that application. Truth is stated, then applied, then is to be obeyed. Let me illustrate.

Here is a truth: Ninety-three million miles away there is a star we call the sun. Its diameter is 109.3 times the diameter of the earth, and its surface is twelve thousand times the earth's surface. Because hydrogen in the sun is heated to twenty-seven million degrees Fahrenheit, it changes into helium, generating tremendous energy. This energy bursts out into space and reaches the earth at the rate of four million horsepower per square mile.

Isn't that exciting? I'm sure you are very encouraged by all this. It's all truth stated.

Now let's go a step further and see some truth applied. Part of the sun's energy is ultraviolet radiation. Ultraviolet radiation beats upon your little epidermis (you may prefer to call it skin) and will do some fascinating things. It may give you what people call a beautiful tan. In that case, on an excursion to the beach you may attract both whistles and friends. On the other hand, if you get too much of this beautiful tan, you may receive something else . . . something like skin cancer.

Now you're sitting up and taking notice.

It's possible for me to spout truckloads of truth about the sun's generating four million horsepower per square mile, while you sit ho-humming the whole thing. But as soon as I mention skin cancer, you say, "What was that? What was that?" Truth stated has become truth applied. But we can't leave it there. We need to take action based on the truth stated and applied.

The sensible action in this case is to avoid excessive, prolonged exposure to ultraviolet radiation. Otherwise you may find yourself with skin cancer; and then, having been unwise in getting it, you might turn to God and complain, "Why did you let this happen to me?" And how might God respond? "I've told you about the sun and its millions of horsepower and about your epidermis and this kind of thing. But you wouldn't listen."

Have you got the picture? Truth stated, truth applied, truth obeyed.

That's the method we'll follow in this book. We'll see what God wants to teach us, ascertain how it is to be applied to our own lives, and determine to obey what we've been shown.

That's the only way to real growth—physical, intellectual, or spiritual. By God's grace, let's determine to do it.

And let's begin today!

I
Christian Beliefs

Learning the Fundamentals

Who Is Jesus?

He is the image of the invisible God,
the firstborn over all creation.
For by him all things were created:
things in heaven and on earth, visible and invisible,
whether thrones or powers or rulers or authorities;
all things were created by him and for him.
He is before all things,
and in him all things hold together.
And he is the head of the body, the church;
he is the beginning and the firstborn from among the dead,
so that in everything he might have the supremacy.
For God was pleased to have all his fullness dwell in him,
and through him to reconcile to himself all things,
whether things on earth or things in heaven,
by making peace through his blood, shed on the cross.
Colossians 1:15-20

For in Christ all the fullness of the Deity
lives in bodily form.
Colossians 2:9

. . . that they may know the mystery of God, namely, Christ,
in whom are hidden all the treasures of wisdom and
knowledge.
Colossians 2:2b-3

The Critical Focus

The prize lay on the table. A new computer! Excitedly its owner cut open the box. Gingerly he took the machine out, studied its manual, and connected all the appropriate wires. Eagerly he flipped on the power switch.

Nothing.

Puzzled, the man switched the computer to "Off" and rechecked all connections. He rounded up a screwdriver and fastened the wires more securely. He reread the relevant portion of the manual. Satisfied that he'd followed directions, once more he flipped the computer to "On."

Nothing.

Confusion turned to anger. What had those salespeople stuck him with? Didn't they say it had been "100 percent tested"?

He was mad. His dealer would hear about this! He reached for the telephone to demand his money back. Just then his little daughter walked into the room.

"Hi, Daddy!" her cheery voice rang out. "What a pretty computer! Can I plug it in?"

In the excitement of a new toy, the man missed the one thing he couldn't afford to forget.

How often that happens to us in our Christian lives! We concentrate on the details of life and neglect Christ. We focus on all kinds of human systems and lose sight of Christ. We listen to all sorts of human authorities and forget that all authority resides in Christ. We get off into the latest ideas and kicks and therapies, and somehow forget that only in Christ do we find all reality.

Paul was constantly warning people on that point. He returned to it again and again and insists that we return there, too.

The whole of the first two chapters of Colossians rings with the truth that all reality is found in Christ. All the fullness of the Godhead dwells in him! He is head over all things! In Christ is to be found all reality! In Christ is to be found centrality of experience! In Christ is to be found all authority!

If anyone ever draws near to confuse you with theories and ideas and approaches and emphases that draw your attention away from Christ, you know that's a person to avoid. Always we must turn our eyes upon Jesus.

That is the word for the church today. Learn Christ! Focus upon him! Meditate upon what he has done!

Forget him, and you're in peril. Remember and honor him, and you will find your life revolutionized.

Isn't that, after all, why he came?

His Majesty, King Jesus

He is the image of the invisible God,
the firstborn over all creation.

Is it easy for you to visualize majesty? If you're an American, it may be more difficult for you than for a Britisher.

When American revolutionaries booted out kings and voted in presidents, they unintentionally helped cloud the nation's sense of majesty. With no monarchs to flaunt their pomp and glory, the idea of regal splendor—of *majesty*—soon faded from memory.

I once heard Jack Hayford tell how a tour of Britain prompted him to write the popular song *Majesty*. He saw the Crown Jewels. He viewed Buckingham Palace. He watched the Guards. He witnessed all the panoply, the majesty, the glory, the magnificence of royalty, and was moved to sit down while still in Britain and write his song.

Don't get me wrong. This isn't a plug for Britain as opposed to America. I'm not foolish enough to do that. You'll stand in line to say, "If it's so great over there, why don't you go back?" No, I won't do that. It's just that sometimes the culture we live in undermines our sense of majesty—even the majesty of our Lord Jesus Christ.

How unfortunate that is! For Christ is the very epitome, the zenith, of what "majesty" is about. Majestic, exalted, lofty, regal, stately, grand—he is all that and more! Paul says Christ "is the image of the invisible God."

Paul means that Christ came to give us a visible expression of a God who is invisible. "He who has seen me has seen the Father," Jesus told his disciples. That is why no one with access to a Bible can claim ignorance of what God is like. Jesus is the image of the invisible God.

But he is more than that. Jesus Christ is a reflection to us of what man was intended to be.

One of the remarkable, enigmatic things about man is his schizophrenia. Creativity oozes from his pores. He can do such magnificent things. Walk around the world with half an eye open, and you'll be awe-struck at the sheer brilliance of mankind.

At the same time, however, we humans are capable of inexplicable cruelty and hostility. We pervert and pollute the most precious and beautiful things in the most dastardly, cowardly way imaginable.

How can these two impulses co-exist? How can mankind be so creative and yet so destructive? Any theory of man that does not account for both is inadequate.

I submit that the only adequate theory sees mankind as having a marred vestige of the divine image. We were created perfect, but we fell.

It's against this idea that we see the magnificence of the Incarnation. Christ came into the world, and against a fallen humanity, stands supreme. In so doing he demonstrates how far we have fallen.

If ever we want to know how we're doing as human beings, we mustn't compare ourselves with ourselves. Instead we must measure ourselves against Jesus, the image of the invisible God . . . the sort of person man was intended to be in the first place.

That leads to something else. Scripture teaches that the Lord Jesus came into the world, died and rose again, then sent his Spirit into the hearts of the redeemed. The objective of the indwelling Spirit is clearly stated more than once in Scripture. It is to work in the hearts of reborn men and women so that ultimately they will be restored to the image of God.

This process will come to its glorious consummation when we stand before the Lord. When we see Jesus, Scripture says we will be like him. What will that mean? Since he is the image of the invisible God, when we see him we will be like him—the image of the invisible God. We will be restored to our full humanity. Christ, through his Spirit, is changing us more and more into his image.

The expression that Jesus is "the firstborn over all creation" has been embraced with great delight by many cultists who deny the deity of the Lord Jesus. Many of you have been visited by Jehovah's Witnesses. Probably you have listened for a long time while they deliver their spiel. I have no doubt they have quoted this verse to you, and in quoting it have said, "There you are! Jesus is the firstborn over all creation. That proves that he is created, which shows quite conclusively he could not possibly be equal with God."

The remarkable thing about these people is the size of their blinkers. For verse 16 immediately goes on to say, "by him all things were created." And verse 17 adds, "he is before all things." And the next verse concludes everything by saying, "in everything he has supremacy."

This verse does not mean that Jesus Christ was the first thing created. That would be to misunderstand what "firstborn" meant in Jewish culture.

The firstborn in a Jewish family was heir in a very special way, with special privileges and responsibilities.

When Paul says Christ is God's firstborn, he means that Jesus rightfully inherits from the Father absolutely everything that was created. *Everything*. Nothing is excluded; nothing is left out. Jesus is "His Majesty" in the ultimate, true, and full sense!

I have never met Queen Elizabeth, even though I was born a British subject. One day, in the maritime provinces of Canada, I found myself staying in the same hotel as the queen.

She walked past me at a distance of about six feet—but that's the limit of my contact with earthly majesty! It would have been inappropriate if I had pushed my way to her side, stretched

23

out my hand, and said, "Hi, Liz, I'm Stuart. You really ought to get to know me."

In fact, you can only speak to the queen if she first speaks to you. You only shake her hand if she extends hers first. You don't push into her presence; you wait to be presented.

No doubt there have been many abuses of monarchy, but the resultant emphasis on uninhibited democracy may have robbed us of a sense of respect, dignity, appropriate restraint, and humility.

This may not be as important as it once was, since most of us will never meet a ruling monarch. But we will meet the King one day—and every day should be lived in the consciousness of that event. Our respect and reverence for him will then be evident and attractive.

I'm glad that Jack Hayford's trip to Britain triggered the writing of *Majesty*. It's a great song. But the royalty and glory and majesty found across the sea, quite frankly, is shabby stuff compared to that of King Jesus. I wonder what Jack might have written had he viewed heaven instead of Buckingham Palace? What a song that would be!

On second thought, maybe not. I've a feeling that when you gaze on the majesty of King Jesus, words simply fail.

(But do you think we could still hum?)

He's in Charge

*For by him all things were created: things in
heaven and on earth, visible and invisible,
whether thrones or powers or rulers or
authorities; all things were created by him and
for him. He is before all things, and in him all
things hold together.*

T he President of the United States of America
wields awesome power as the Commander-in-
Chief of all U. S. military forces. Even he, however, can't do just
what he likes with that power. The sphere of his operation is the
constitution. When he takes his oath as president, he pledges to
operate within the confines of the constitution.

In the same way, God the Father has chosen to use all his
mighty power in creation exclusively in and through Christ. The
president operates in and through the constitution. The Father
operates in and through his Son. Jesus is the sphere of all creation.
Not only that, he is the agent of creation. Beyond that, absolutely
everything that was created in him and through him was created
exclusively for him.

Paul says it doesn't matter whether the things created are
in heaven or on earth, whether they're visible or invisible—everything was created for him. Thrones, powers, rulers, authorities—
all things were created through him and for him.

That assumes that Jesus existed before anything was
created. And that's exactly what Paul means. Far from being part

of creation and far from creation being part of him, Jesus is before all things. John says the same thing in John 1:1: "In the beginning was the Word, and the Word was with God, and the Word was God." Before anything was made, John says, the Word was continually in existence.

While that's a powerful statement, it's also hard to get a handle on.

We can get a handle on the Incarnation. We love little babies in mangers. We love the idea of everyone bowing down and worshiping before the manger. We can get a handle on that.

We can get a handle on Jesus the man, that Christ was horribly beaten and terribly maltreated and awfully betrayed and desperately deserted and cruelly scourged and viciously crucified. We can get a handle on that.

We can even get excited about the idea of Jesus' rising from the dead in a resurrection body and appearing to his disciples.

The thing we have a hard time handling is that this incarnate, rejected, crucified, maligned, spat-upon Jesus existed before anything was created.

Unless we do begin to think of him in those terms, however, the significance of his incarnation and death and resurrection will elude us. It was the pre-existent One who laid aside his glory, assumed our humanity, and stepped down into our life.

When it says he is before all things, it doesn't say "before all things were created, he *was*." That would be good grammar but bad theology. Jesus does not operate on the basis of tenses as we do. We think in terms of past and present and future. And if we're really into it, we think in terms of imperfect and pluperfect and perfect and all kinds of other incomprehensibles we forgot in school before we learned them. As far as Jesus is concerned, it's very simple. He has only one tense—the present. Before all things were created, he *is*. He is the pre-existent, eternal one.

That explains his superior status. Nothing created can possibly rank ahead of him. This is why idolatry is so detestable, for idolaters value the created thing more highly than the Creator. Idolatry is elevating created things above the One by, in, through, and for whom all things were created.

Then notice Paul says "in him all things hold together." Peter tells us that the same hand that brought things into being will control them until he terminates all things. It will be true to say, as far as creation is concerned, that Christ perpetuates all things until he is ready to terminate all things. But when Paul says Jesus holds all things together, he doesn't just mean that Christ perpetuates what he initiated. He means that, in some way, Jesus maintains and sustains every created thing.

Sometimes when I'm preaching I get all worked up. And on occasion when I've got all worked up I have banged my hand on our solid oak pulpit. I assure you it is solid, and that its edges are very sharp.

Occasionally I rap my knuckles on one of those sharp edges, and immediately thereafter my congregation thinks, "Wow, is he preaching up a storm!" No, I am not. I'm in agony. There is nothing quite so solid as a solid oak pulpit, particularly when you rap your knuckles on it and you are only halfway through your second point. In other words, another forty minutes to go in torment.

I do take some comfort in discovering that solid matter is not really solid at all. It's really made up of space, with a few little things whizzing around inside it. I confess I don't understand it. But I understand on good authority that everything we regard as solid is in fact mostly space. If we could just figure out how to get rid of your space, we could get many more people into the nation's sanctuaries, and thereby solve all building problems.

The point is, that which we regard as solid is actually made up of infinitesimally small objects held together by space. And the space is held together by some indescribable, indefinable power.

Now, of course, some very smart people discovered the atom. And they said, "that's what we are made up of." But then some very, very smart people said, "Ah ha! The atom is made up of all sorts of smaller things." In fact, you can split an atom and discover all kinds of other things—protons, neutrons, croutons, what have you.

All these things are held together by some strange, powerful force. "If," said some bright person, "we can split the atom and release its indefinable force, we would have at our disposal unspeakable energy and power."

Who Is Jesus?

All the time they are probing further and further. What they're discovering is less and less, bound together by the most phenomenal power. And nobody on earth knows what it is.

All things, in some strange way, hold together. To the best of my knowledge, there is absolutely no reason why you, being made mostly of space, should not just disintegrate. Me, too. What a mess that would be.

But all our universe is held together, and scientific minds all over the planet are seeking to understand why. Physicists are looking into it. Mathematicians are puzzling over it. They're all trying to figure it out.

Could it be that the clue is found, of all places, in the Bible? It says that "in him all things hold together."

Do you begin to get a glimmer of the mind-boggling dimensions of King Jesus? Don't worry if you don't understand this. Join the club—nobody understands it. Wouldn't it be disappointing if you thoroughly understood deity? That would mean deity was no bigger than your mental capability, and with all due respect to your mental capability, you can keep that kind of deity for yourself.

Fortunately, we don't have to settle for some little, puny, inconsequential, feeble and impotent god. We have King Jesus! Long may he boggle our minds!

We could even have a motto: *Semper Boggled*—forever boggled. The marines may not like it, but they don't have to. The Jesus I know can take care of himself. So let's hear it again: *Semper Boggled!*

It kind of grows on you, doesn't it?

The Supreme Commander

*And he is the head of the body, the church; he is
the beginning and the firstborn from among the
dead, so that in everything he might have the
supremacy.*

Some time ago I was in Brazil. I went down with Jill for some meetings. While there I made inquiries about seeing a soccer match. An Englishman just grieves over not being able to see soccer when he's living in a foreign land, but if you can go to Brazil, that's the next best thing. They told me there was only one game in the whole of Brazil that weekend.

"Don't tell me that, where is it?" I asked.

I was taken to the window of the house where I was staying and directed toward a stadium just outside: "There," they said.

"You mean there's only one game in Brazil, and it's there?"

"Yes."

"What is it?"

"It's our Super Bowl, or the equivalent."

"Is there the remotest chance that we can get tickets? Could you please get me a ticket to see that game?"

"What a relief! What a relief!" they exclaimed. "We'd all got tickets, and we didn't think we could go because you'd want to have a meeting."

"Oh, no, no! Jill can do the meeting," I explained. "We'll go to the game."

Our excitement grew when we entered the vast stadium and began to feel the thrill of the Super Bowl of Brazilian soccer. Both teams came out, and my friends nudged me. "You see the center forward playing for that team down there? He's a member of our church," they said.

We took our seats, and the game began. The teams were evenly matched; neither could get an advantage over the other. Near the end of the game there was still no score. Americans would hate it. No score at all. A basketball game by then would have been 124-122. But nil, nil in soccer.

Suddenly the right winger cut away, beat his man, crossed the ball, and our man came right down the middle with a phenomenal burst of speed. He gauged his run until his head intersected with the ball, a fabulous piece of judgment. He came between two defenders, headed up the ball, brought it down on his chest, held his arms out not to touch it, and with his chest brought the ball down onto his left knee. He flipped it up onto his right foot, took it around a man, and hit it on the half volley with his left foot. It went straight into the top corner of the net. That made the score 1-0, enough to win the game.

Why do I explain all that to you? Because it demonstrates just how wonderfully coordinated the human body is. How was he able to gauge the ball's arrival? How was he able to gauge what height it would be, what speed it was going, or how part of his body should meet it? And how could he determine a way to get it between two defenders, take it on his head, bounce it on his chest, flip it from his knee onto the other foot, take it around one man, and hit it with another foot quicker than you can explain the whole thing?

The answer is coordination and control.

Now, the church is described in many different ways, but perhaps the model we are most familiar with is the idea of it as a body. We all know what a body does and how it functions. In this passage, Paul says that Jesus Christ controls and coordinates members of the fellowship and holds the church together as a head controls a body.

Christ is the head of the body, the church, and the church can be a disaster or it can be phenomenal. The key to making it phenomenal is to allow the Lord Jesus to be the controlling factor of its individual members. Each member must allow Jesus' Spirit to direct each one to be what he wants them to be and to do what he wants them to do. There can be none of this individual stuff, but instead a tremendous sense of his over- arching control and wise coordination. Jesus is utterly magnificent in the church.

But then Paul goes on to say this: "He is the beginning, the firstborn from among the dead." Here is the idea of firstborn again. It does not mean he was the first to rise from the dead. We know that isn't true. He raised some from the dead himself. But he was the firstborn from the dead in the sense that when he arose from the dead, he could never die again.

In being the firstborn, he was heir to eternal life. As heir, he can dispense it to all. He, in his resurrection, would make it possible for us to be raised into newness of life. Hence the idea of beginning.

When we are raised into newness of life by the risen Christ, that's a new beginning. We're alive in the power of his resurrection. He becomes the dynamic of our life.

So what's the church? The church is a group of people indwelt by the life of the risen Christ, raised in newness of life in him, controlled by him as head, coordinated into a cohesive body in which his Spirit moves in his ancient ways. Jesus is utterly magnificent in the church.

Now the church, unfortunately, sometimes gets a long way away from Jesus. As soon as it does, it becomes not the body, but the corpse.

The thing that makes the church the church is not the preacher, nor the elders, nor its people. The thing that makes the church the church is the head, Christ, who is powerfully at work in individual lives. The church is utterly dependent upon him. He is magnificent. I think Paul is running out of gas here because he sort of grabs the whole thing together and says, "So in everything he is supreme."

Who Is Jesus?

Do you remember the time of Operation Overlord—the Normandy invasion of World War II? Until that time the armies of the Allies served under various commanders. But now they came together to attack the stronghold of Nazi Germany. It was necessary that there be a Supreme Commander. You couldn't have the British commanded by the British any longer, or the Americans by an American, or the Australians by an Australian, or the New Zealanders by a New Zealander, or the South Africans by a South African. Free French, Belgians, Norwegians—you couldn't have them all doing their own thing. There had to be a Supreme Commander, and he was chosen. Dwight Eisenhower was that man.

He did a wonderful job. But with all due respect to Mr. Eisenhower, he was not the Supreme Commander. That title is reserved for the one who is King of kings and Lord of lords, that in everything he might have the supremacy.

Now remember the point of all of this. If we are to enjoy life in the kingdom, if we are to enjoy the life of believers, it is in relationship to the King. And if our relationship to the King is to be right, our understanding of him must be constantly enlarged.

That's the best kind of enlarging there is. Many of you may be worrying about enlarging of other sorts—around the waist, hips, or thighs, for example. We won't talk about that. You never need to worry about enlarging overmuch in your apprehension of the Lord Jesus, however. Learn as much as you can, as long as you can. Enlarge your understanding! After eighty years, you'll still be skin and bones in proportion to the amount there is to devour.

Just think of it—mounds and mounds of luscious, delectable truth about King Jesus, inviting you to sit down and indulge. Enlarge yourself in your knowledge of Christ the King! It's the one area where dieting is downright harmful to your health!

Putting Things Together Again

For God was pleased to have all his fullness dwell in him, and through him to reconcile to himself all things, whether things on earth or things in heaven, by making peace through his blood, shed on the cross.

Have you ever come to know and admire someone of great gifts and ability, only later to discover you didn't know the half of it?

Something like that apparently happened late in 1987 to film critics across the country. Many thought of director Steven Spielberg as a one-dimensional talent, a fellow who put out cute, wholesome fantasies (like *E. T., the Extraterrestrial*). His pictures may not mean much, the critics said, but they're great fun.

Then the Christmas season rolled around, and Spielberg released a film titled *Empire of the Sun*. It told the story of a young English boy interned by the Japanese from 1941 to 1945 in occupied China. The critics were astonished—Spielberg wasn't thought capable of creating a thoughtful picture like *Empire*. One critic, Ted Mahar of the Portland, Ore., *Oregonian*, wrote:

> *Empire of the Sun* was my favorite film of the year, easily. Steven Spielberg's epic realization of J. G. Ballard's . . . novel is a greater leap than I thought possible for him.

Mahar knew Spielberg could make films that appealed to the child in each of us; he didn't think he could make a film like *Empire*. When the critic emerged from the theater to write his critique of Spielberg's film, however, he came out with a wholly different and enlarged view of the man behind the picture. Mahar had no idea how great Spielberg's talent was. He came away astonished at what he saw.

If you take Mahar's astonishment and multiply it by a billion billion, you will get a glimmer of the awe and amazement that Jesus prompted in the apostle Paul.

Paul knew that Jesus is magnificent in the creation.

He knew that Jesus is magnificent in the church.

But finally he saw him in fuller glory: Jesus is magnificent in the Christian. His greatness is magnified in what he does in the lives and hearts of the redeemed.

When Jesus came to earth as the God-Man, God was pleased for all his fullness to dwell in Christ. Everything that makes God, God, was present in Christ.

That had special significance for the church at Colossae. When Paul wrote his letter, the church was battling some heretics who quite probably were teaching a doctrine that eventually would develop into something called "gnosticism." This heresy nearly demolished the church of the second century.

Gnostics stressed two ideas. First, they taught that to really understand spiritual things you had to be initiated in a special way. The gnostics controlled the way. "We have all the truth," they said. "Do it our way or forget it." If you had not gained this special enlightenment, this special knowledge, you hadn't even gotten to square one.

Second, they believed that matter was evil and spirit was good. Therefore God, who is Spirit, could have nothing to do with the creation, which was material and evil. Spirit and matter could never touch.

This was a problem for these men, since they wanted contact with God. They got around the problem by imagining a whole set of intermediary "emanations" between spirit and matter. When someone became enlightened, when he or she had this special experience, all the emanations came together and the lucky one received the fullness of the whole thing. And they shouted, "Eureka, I've arrived!"

Paul came around and said, "No, that's not the way to go. Matter is not evil; all things were created by Christ and through him and for him. You don't need all kinds of intermediary emanations between God and man. In Christ you have everything you need. When Jesus came, incarnate in him was everything needed for true spiritual experience."

That is profound. We need to be reminded that God was pleased to have all his fullness dwell in Christ, and that all his fullness is available to us.

There is more. Paul says that this one in whom dwells everything needed for spiritual satisfaction is the one through whom God sought to reconcile all things to himself.

When Paul says God will reconcile to himself all things, he doesn't say God is going to reconcile all *people*. He doesn't say everyone will end up in heaven because God is neat and cute and kind and gentle. To believe that is to deny Scripture. Salvation *is* available to all. The death of Christ *is* efficacious for all. But not all will respond. He does not reconcile all people to himself. He reconciles *in Christ* all things to himself.

What does that mean?

Let's back up a little. When man fell, society began to disintegrate. When society began to disintegrate, ecology got out of whack. When ecology got out of whack, all kinds of things went wrong. As a result, we have loads of tension and disease and hurt and heartache. In short, when mankind fell, everything came unglued.

That will all change when God puts things back together in a new heaven and a new earth, where Christ will be King of kings and Lord of lords. At that time he will reconcile all things to himself. And in so doing everything will be the opposite of out of whack. What's that? In whack. All things will be in whack.

Paul wasn't quite through yet. After having gone off into the lofty heights, he came down with a bump to earth. And what a bump! For he says all this is possible because Christ made peace through his blood, shed on the cross. Having given us a glorious vista of the magnificence of the Lord Jesus, he says we appreciate it only to the degree we see this pre-existent one laying aside his glory, assuming our humanity, dying our death, giving his life, and shedding his blood for the remission of sin in order that we might be reconciled to God. That's quite a resume!

Are you, personally, at a place in your life where you appreciate who Jesus is and what he has done for you? I'm not asking if you have accepted Christ as your Savior. I hope that you have, and that if you haven't, you will. What I'm wondering about now is the depth of your affection for Jesus himself, as your friend, brother, Savior, God, and Lord.

Have you told him recently what he means to you? Have you pondered his willing sacrifice on your behalf? Have you thanked him for his care of you? Do you brag about him to others?

Take some time, right now, to treasure this Jesus. Take a moment to talk to him. Not because you have to, or because guilt makes you, *but because he is worthy!* Jesus is magnificent in the Christian—that's you, and that's me.

Let's thank him for it!

Down to Earth

For in Christ all the fullness of the Deity
lives in bodily form.

This statement in Colossians 2:9, a restatement of what we saw in 1:19, ought to be so heavily underlined in your Bible that it comes right through to the leather binding. It is something of profound significance. If you forget that in Christ is found all the fullness of deity in bodily form, you will have an impossibly shallow view of his reality. If you have an impossibly shallow view of the reality of Christ, your relationship with him will suffer—and the essence of your life is relationship with Christ.

All that goes to make God, God, is invested in the Lord Jesus Christ. If there is anything you want to know about God, look to Christ. If it is truth you are interested in, if it is his life you are interested in, if it is righteousness you are interested in, look to Christ. All those things emanate from the very being and the nature and the essence of God, and are found in Christ. If you want to find them, look to Christ.

That's not where people today look for them. When men and women search for truth today, where do they look? All over the place. When they look for life, where do they go? All over the place. When they hunt for what's right, where do they run? All over the place. Even believers!

Paul brings us back to square one and says, "No, all the fullness of Deity dwells in bodily form in Christ. All that makes God what he is, all that is good and right and true and real, is demonstrated in Christ. Don't wander from him in your search for reality."

All the fullness of deity lives "in bodily form," Paul says. Notice his emphasis on God's fullness (which is spiritual) residing in Christ's body (which is physical).

Remember the Colossian heresy, which taught that spiritual is good and physical is bad, that the two could never mix any more than good and evil could mix?

Paul insists that God's Spirit is found in Christ, as man, in bodily form.

This emphasis on the physical reminds us of the Incarnation, of the crucifixion, the ascension, and the glorification.

When we think of the baby Jesus in a manger, we think of God in bodily form. We remember that God took the initiative to come and dwell with us. *Emmanuel*, he was called, "God with us."

When we look at the cross, we see a man writhing in agony, in physical torture. God, in whom all fullness is to be found in Christ in bodily form, bore our sins.

When we see the empty tomb, we learn that this loving God was raised again, and in his resurrection body ascended to the Father's right hand where he sat down and even today makes intercession for us.

In the Incarnation, this wonderful God came to be with us.

In the crucifixion, this wonderful God chose to die for us.

In the resurrection, this wonderful God gave us life.

In the ascension, this wonderful God gave us hope and access to the Father.

When we think of all the fullness in bodily form, we rejoice that this wonderful God—in whom truth and righteousness and reality and life are to be found—died for us, lived among us, and now constantly prays for us.

This is the basis of our faith. Never let yourself be diverted from it!

Be warned that deceivers will try to deflect your attention from Christ. They will pervert the gospel and oppose the Lordship of Christ.

Beware! Be instructed! Remember that all reality is found in Christ. Remember that this Christ is the One with whom we have a living relationship.

It has often been said that Christianity is not so much a religion as a relationship. This is easy to say, and accordingly is often misunderstood. The point of it is this: The major religions of the world are attempts by man to follow the teachings of a dead prophet. Christianity, on the other hand, is the unspeakable privilege of a redeemed man or woman living in union with a risen, living, exalted Lord.

The essence of Christianity is not found in trying to follow the teachings of a dead Jesus. The essence of Christianity is that you and I can be related to God through Jesus, the divine Son of God who was incarnate, was crucified, is risen, and lives in the power of an endless life.

That is why the rest of Colossians 2:9-13 is riddled with the expressions "in him" and "with him." It is *in* Christ—in relationship to him—and *with* him—in relationship with him—that genuine spiritual experience is to be found.

It's possible to find all kinds of spiritual experiences outside of Christ. People do it all the time. But if you want the real thing, the thing that satisfies and fulfills and strengthens and completes and comforts and delights, you'll never find it until you search for it, grasp it, and rest in it in Christ.

In Christ, "all the fullness of the Deity lives in bodily form."

All the boundless power and strength that "fullness" implies is available to every believer in Christ. Are you taking advantage of it?

I've got some homework for you. Take out a pen or a marker. Open your Bible to Colossians 2:9. Underline that verse so heavily that the ink comes through to the other side.

Who Is Jesus?

It's a truth you can put feet to!

When I was a small boy, my father made me a pair of stilts. I quickly learned to walk on them and even, for some strange reason, practiced until I could get around on just one stilt.

There was a bully in our neighborhood who intimidated all the kids, me included. One day he knocked me off my stilts and proceeded to jump on them in order to smash them. I can still remember the helpless feeling as I stood by, screaming at him to stop, but knowing I could do nothing.

What I didn't know was that my dad was watching from the window. He rushed out, grabbed the bully, returned my stilts to me, and told the bully what to expect if he came around again!

My despair turned to delight, defeat changed into victory, assurance replaced insecurity. It had nothing to do with me, and everything to do with my father.

Life can be a bully, and it is all too easy for us to stand helplessly by, screaming—unless, of course, we have learned who Christ is, what he offers, and are related to him by faith. When all that is true of us, the bully has no choice but to flee.

The Mystery Solved

*... that they may know the mystery of God,
namely, Christ, in whom are hidden all the
treasures of wisdom and knowledge.*

There's something tantalizing about a secret. Secrets have an almost irresistible power to arouse our curiosity, to whet our thirst for a bit of information no one else has.

Do you remember how as a child, one of the most irritating taunts anyone could flip your way was—in that awful sing-song voice—"I know something you don't know!"

Many cults use the lure of secrets to charm the unwary into their web of lies. "We know the hidden way to God," they whisper. "Join us and learn the secret. Nobody else can help you. Nobody else knows what it is. We alone have the answer. Wouldn't you like to join us? Wouldn't you like to be part of an exclusive and favored circle? Come on inside. We can't talk out here."

Something just like that was going on in Paul's time. In those days "mystery religions" were sprouting up all over. People outside their cliques hadn't a clue what went on inside. People on the inside believed they understood the secrets of the universe; its mysteries were no mystery to them.

Paul borrows that little word "mystery" here and uses it for his own purposes. When he writes about a mystery, he's not talking about an Agatha Christie style mystery where God is sitting up there spinning a tale intended to confuse. What he's saying is, "Look, do you really want to understand how the universe is put together? Do you really want to know the mystery of God? Then come to Christ. Christ is the mystery of God; Christ is the One who unveils God. Commit yourself to Christ, and you'll begin to understand what you never understood before—who God really is."

Is that something you'd like? Would getting a clearer vision of God meet a desperate need in your life? If so, you need to know Christ more fully.

You needn't join some secretive, select clique huddled off in some corner to do so. You don't need some secret initiation rite or a specially trained tutor to learn Jesus. The Christ you need to know was crucified publicly, resurrected in power, written about in the Gospels, and is available to anyone who calls upon him. The mystery of God has been openly revealed in Jesus. Paul said as much in Colossians 1:28: "We *proclaim* him, admonishing *every man* and teaching *every man* with all wisdom, that we may present *every man* complete in Christ."

This Christ, who is the mystery of God, is the One in whom are hidden all the treasures of wisdom and knowledge. What a prize for people searching out truth!

Have you noticed that this search goes on all the time? We're constantly encouraged to look into all areas of knowledge. There's an explosion of it. The minute you write an encyclopedia, it's out of date. The folks over at the Encyclopedia Britannica think it's great. If ever you get on their enrollment, you'll get books coming every few minutes. You'll never have time to read them, but they keep coming.

When we look into all these areas of knowledge, it's easy to become confused. It's possible to get sidetracked.

Some people say, "Wow, look at all this stuff! I'm going to get off into these areas," and they forget Christ.

Others recognize that danger and say, "Well, I won't study anything, then. I'll just study Christ."

There's a balance we've got to maintain. All truth is God's

truth, but what determines whether it's true is its agreement with Christ. As I move into psychology or as I study philosophy or as I look into cosmology or as I get into futurology, I test everything by whether it's skewed with Christ.

If what I'm discovering in philosophy is flatly contradictory to Christ, then that philosophy is wrong.

If what I'm studying in psychology contravenes what Christ taught, then I put that psychology on the side of the plate.

The bottom line is this: If all the treasures of wisdom and knowledge are found in Christ, then anything that opposes Christ is wrong.

Christ is the One from whom all things emanate. He is the One by, for, and through whom all things were created. He is the One who ultimately will rule and reign when everything is made subject to him.

Because this is true, we've got to encourage each other to know him. In knowing him we'll have the mystery of God opened up to us—not to keep to ourselves as some closely guarded secret, but as a treasure to enrich those around us.

And here's the kicker. You can tell this secret without spoiling the fun, and share this treasure without making it shrink.

You won't find that kind of bounty anywhere else in the universe.

So What?

Therefore ...

What a way to begin a chapter. You've only just begun, and already I'm cheating. You can't see where? Let me point it out to you.

You see that little word at the head of the page? It's the first word in Colossians 2:16: "Therefore ..." It's a great little word. Very useful, too. In fact, it's so useful that I'm using it for my own purposes. Since we're starting out each chapter with a verse from Colossians, and since this little word is exactly what I need at this point, I'm ripping it out of context and depositing it here.

Don't get too concerned, though. I'm using it just like the apostle Paul did—to explain the relevance of a profound truth. You see, we need to get over the "so what" hump. It's quite possible for a writer to have a marvelous time spouting out theology by the mile, while those out in the workaday world are trying to pay debts and raise kids and handle bosses and deal with all kinds of nasty, hard, difficult relationships. So while the writer—me—is having a marvelous time with his theology, his readers sit there impatiently asking, "so what?"

Who Is Jesus?

Some try to get over this hump by starting with where people are and leaving it at that, never bringing Jesus into the discussion. We can't do that. The "so what" of Paul's teaching about Jesus is very simple. Let me suggest three things.

First, if Jesus Christ is head of creation and head of the church—and he is!—then we don't have the freedom to do what the gnostics were doing. We can't say, "Well, one part of my life is sacred and the rest of it is secular. Sunday morning I'll act religious, but the rest of the week is mine. I'll keep my spiritual experience in a watertight compartment while living the vast majority of my life in the secular realm. I'll make sure the two never connect."

Jesus refuses to give us that option. He created all things. He is the head of the church. Our spiritual experience, our natural experience, our material experience—all come from him and come under his lordship. *Therefore,* we are not free to talk about "the sacred" and "the secular." We must bring all areas of our life under his lordship.

Second, if Christ is supreme, he is absolutely sufficient. He created the world and keeps it going. We worship the creator of all things, the one who upholds everything by the word of his power. *Therefore,* he can work in *our* lives, too.

Do we believe that? Too often we think, "He can handle the universe, but not me. The universe must bow to him, but I don't need to bow myself." What foolishness!

Fortunately, Jesus doesn't allow us to carry on like that for long. He is supreme, and he is sufficient. He is the King, and sooner or later we will be called into his presence to acknowledge the fact. How much better to do so with joy!

Third, Jesus is the unifying and unique factor of all existence. There is nothing we can add to him. Nothing. *Therefore,* don't try. As he is the unifying factor, we can keep nothing from him. He is the King of kings and Lord of lords, and everything we have—everything—belongs ultimately to him.

Charles Wesley was certainly right. Pondering that first Christmas morning, he wrote of the infant Jesus, "God contracted to a span, incomprehensibly made man."

That Almighty God should become a helpless baby is surely incomprehensible. How could it be otherwise? But oh, the riches that are ours through his incarnation, death, and resurrection!

"God contracted to a span, incomprehensibly made man." Only when we accept this and revel in it do we begin to see the significance of the magnificence of King Jesus. And only then do we begin to really live! *Therefore* . . .

Hail, King Jesus!

Working Out

1. Colossians 1:15-20 gives at least 10 distinctive traits about Christ. Take out a sheet of paper and divide it into two columns. In the left hand column, write down each trait you can find. In the right hand column, write down at least two ways in which each trait should affect your life. Make this as practical as you can. For example:

Christ's Traits

Jesus is the image of God.

My Response

1. I need to spend time in the Gospels to see who God is and what he's like.

2. If I want to be godly, I not only must know what Jesus is like, but must do the kinds of things he did.

Jesus is the head of the church.

1. If I want to be connected to Jesus in a real way, I've got to be involved in the church.

2. In spite of my church's faults, if Jesus is the head, something good must be happening in it. I've got to find out what it is and encourage it.

2. Read the passage once again and note how often Paul talks about "physical" kinds of things. He writes, for example, of "created" things (1:16), of the "church" (1:18), of Christ's "blood" (1:20), of Christ's "cross" (1:20), of Christ's "physical body" (1:22), etc.

Take some time to ask yourself, "how is my faith being worked out in my physical world? Do I see my job or my children or my commitments as hindrances to my spiritual growth—they're only earthly, after all—or as great opportunities to increase my spiritual growth?"

Write down at least five ways in which the things that surround you physically can be used to help you grow spiritually.

Second Wind

1. Philippians 2:5-11
   Which aspects of Christ's experience can we imitate, and which aspects belong to him alone?

2. 1 Peter 2:18-25
   How did Christ bear up under his suffering and not retaliate against his tormentors? Can we do likewise?

3. Hebrews 1:1-3:6
   Taking full account of all this passage has to say about Christ, how does it make you feel that he calls all believers his "brothers" (2:11-12)?

4. The Gospel of Mark
   If you had to pick five words to describe Jesus as he appears in the Gospel of Mark, what would they be?

5. Revelation 5:1-14
   What is the natural reaction of those who see Jesus face to face?

What's a Christian?

*Paul . . . to the holy and faithful brothers in Christ
at Colossae:*
Colossians 1:2

*Once you were alienated from God
and were enemies in your minds because of your evil behavior.
But now he has reconciled you
by Christ's physical body through death
to present you holy in his sight,
without blemish and free from accusation . . .*
Colossians 1:21-22

*. . . and you have been given fullness in Christ,
who is the head over every power and authority.
In him you were also circumcised,
in the putting off of the sinful nature,
not with a circumcision done by the hands of men
but with the circumcision done by Christ,
having been buried with him in baptism
and raised with him through your faith in the power of God,
who raised him from the dead.
When you were dead in your sins
and in the uncircumcision of your sinful nature,
God made you alive with Christ.
He forgave us all our sins,
having canceled the written code, with its regulations,
that was against us and that stood opposed to us;
he took it away, nailing it to the cross.*
Colossians 2:10-14

A Full Life

here are some clubs in Milwaukee I've never been in, and there are many, many clubs in Milwaukee of which I'm not a part. In fact, I am not member of any club in Milwaukee, mostly because I don't want to be. Some of them won't have me; I'm not qualified. And I really don't care because I have some great news for you: I qualify for the greatest club in the world. Let me tell you about my membership.

I am a member of the Saints in Light, and I have available to me all the inheritance of God. The exciting thing about it is that I qualify as a member for that club, not because of anything at all that I did, but because Jesus took me by the hand, introduced me to that elite group, and recommended me for membership. Boy, am I thankful!

Do you know what I discovered? I discovered that my life has changed because I can live in light of the fact that I am a member of this select, elite club of saints who enjoy the inheritance of light, a light so powerful that it banishes all darkness. God touched my life and gave me the light of knowledge of himself, casting out the darkness and ignorance and ignominy and shame.

He touched my sin and washed it all away and set me apart for himself. Yes, I'm a member of the Saints in Light, and I'm thankful.

I'm thankful not only for qualification, but for emancipation, too. You see, I not only have been qualified to share in the inheritance of the Saints in Light, but Christ has rescued me from the dominion of darkness. Spiritual ignorance no longer reigns in my life; I am no longer gripped with disgrace and guilt and darkness.

God moved into my life, and through Christ's death and resurrection I was delivered from ignorance and evil, had my eyes opened to the truth, and was rescued from all the things I was ashamed of. He blotted out those things, set me free, and gave me a new life. I've been emancipated! When you know that, you're grateful.

The movie *The Killing Fields* was based on the true story of a *New York Times* reporter working in Cambodia during a time of awful bloodshed. This reporter had a Cambodian assistant who was captured by the Khmer Rouge, a Marxist, totalitarian regime known for its desperate cruelty. The movie is really about his awful suffering.

It's not a movie for the squeamish. Eventually the assistant escapes, lives in fear of his life, and runs from one adventure to another. In one scene he sinks in a bog that he discovers is made entirely of rotting flesh, skulls, and skeletons. He almost dies. He flees from one horror to another, escaping each time by the skin of his teeth.

One day he comes through the jungle and walks to the rise of a hill. He looks down and sees the border below him. He sees a little refugee camp and a hospital with a red cross on a white field. The music starts up and a new light comes to his face as only the movies can portray it. He's free!

When I look at my life, I understand that Christ has qualified me to be a Saint in Light. When I look at my life and understand that God has emancipated me from the power of darkness, I am thankful. I don't need to chase after every new thrill that comes along. I don't need to spend my time and energy looking for something else. What do they matter? I am so thankful because of my new situation.

I've become a member of the kingdom of the Son of his love, and I'm thankful for the redemption I have in him. Redemption means freedom from sin's power, it means forgiveness of sin's record, and I know it was purchased for me by Jesus on the cross.

I shall never forget what he did. I shall never forget what it cost him. And I shall never stop being grateful to him. Somebody has said that the theology of Christianity is grace, the ethic of Christianity is gratitude. I couldn't have said it better myself. When I understand what God in his grace has done for me, the spontaneous response of my heart is thankfulness.

Is it fulfillment you want? You'll only find it in a rich relationship to the living God.

Is it satisfaction you crave? You'll only find it in a life dedicated to loving devotion to God.

When you're fully involved in doing good, in trying to please God, a full life is the natural result. Do that, and you'll find yourself living a winsomely, distinctively attractive Christian life.

It's called fulfillment. And it's found in a living, growing relationship with Christ.

Making Progress

*Once you were alienated from God and were
enemies in your minds because of your evil
behavior.*

When John Bunyan, the Bedfordshire Tinker, was thrown into jail, he didn't sit there bemoaning his fate. He decided to write a book. The book that he wrote is probably the most famous allegory in the English language. *Pilgrim's Progress* describes the journey of a man who, with a great load of sin on his back, was making his way from the slough of despond to the celestial city.

The apostle Paul uses a similar approach to the Colossians in this passage of Scripture. While he doesn't use the picturesque, dramatic form that Bunyan does, still he brings people to an understanding of where they were in the slough of despond and how they're heading toward the celestial city.

In exactly the same way, we need to be thinking in terms of where we were and where we are and where we're going, and how we can get there from here. The Christian life is a progression. It is a journey, something we are working on and are having worked out in us day after day. I want to talk about getting there from here.

Now, Christians sometimes tend to be a little hard on themselves. They've got high aspirations; they know what they're aiming to be. But they get terribly discouraged. They feel they're not getting anywhere.

There's a simple antidote for that—remember where you were, and compare that with where you are. You'll probably find loads of encouraging things.

On the other hand, there are some Christians who get complacent. "Hey, that's where I used to be, and look where I am now—I've arrived!" they say. But God responds, "No, not quite. Remember where you're going, and realize there's a whole lot more that needs to be done in your life."

We need balance in our conception of the Christian walk. We need to think in terms of where we were, where we are, and where we're going.

Remember that this passage of Scripture was written to believers in Jesus Christ. The tenses, therefore, may not apply to you, but pay close attention, for much of what's here may be of great help.

"Once you were alienated from God and were enemies in your minds because of your evil behavior," Paul writes. He says Christians recognize that once they were alienated or estranged from God.

That has enormous implications, for the Bible teaches that people were made by God for God, and that the only way they can live truly human lives is in relationship to God.

If a man or woman is made by God for God to live in union with God, but somehow has lost God, then clearly something's terribly amiss. There's an enormous hole in that life.

These holes express themselves in differing ways. Some people are blatantly antagonistic to God. "You were alienated from God and were enemies in your minds," Paul writes.

That doesn't mean merely that we argued intellectually against God. It means that our attitudes were antagonistic toward him. We blasphemed his name. We shook our fists in his face. We denied his existence. Sometimes we lived in ways clearly and brazenly opposed to everything he said. We were alienated from the life of God and were fully antagonistic toward him.

The antagonism of others is more covert. They simply disregard God. They regard him as irrelevant, as something considerably less than the center of their lives.

Whether the antagonism is overt or covert, failing to acknowledge God as God is a hostile position. Christians can testify that at one stage in their experience, they were alienated from God, antagonistic and hostile in attitude.

Can you recall your own life before you met Christ? Do you remember the feeling of alienation, the sense of restlessness? Do you recall the inner emptiness, the desperate search for satisfaction and self-fulfillment?

The old theologians had an explanation for this. They said there is a God-shaped vacuum inside each of us which can't be filled with anything but God himself. We're born alienated from God, and we'll only be fulfilled and satisfied when God himself steps into our lives to fill that God-shaped blank.

When God is not there to fill the void, evil breaks out. Paul says that unbelievers are active in evil behavior. "Once you were alienated from God and were enemies in your mind because of your evil behavior," he writes. Those who are antagonistic to God, either covertly or overtly, clearly are not living to please God. They are earning his wrath.

It may be that some of us can look back to lives that were inexpressibly evil. We lived as we pleased and couldn't care less who got hurt. Or it may be that our lives before Christ didn't seem so evil. "Hey, listen," we might say, "I was never like that. I was just a normal, decent, law-abiding citizen."

The problem is that our standards of decency and law are such that it is quite possible to be a decent, law-abiding citizen, and still be considered evil in God's eyes. We need to measure our behavior, not against normally accepted principles, but against what God has said in his Word.

Christians have no problem agreeing with Paul's words. They say, "Yes, I remember when I was alienated from God. Yes, I remember when I was active in evil behavior. I am not proud of it. But I am so glad that something happened to change my condition. I'm so glad that Jesus came into my life, turned it around, and set me on a new course. I am no longer what I once was."

Can you make that kind of declaration? If you can, then I'd like to encourage you to continue growing in the faith you've embraced. It only gets better.

And if you can't, I'd like to say there's no time like the present to get started with God. Your chest is no place for a vacuum.

Back Where I Belong

But now he has reconciled you by Christ's
physical body through death to present you holy
in his sight, without blemish and free from
accusation.

Suppose you lived years ago in a wild, sparsely popu-
lated portion of the old west. Suppose you had
moved there with your family to transform the inhospitable coun-
tryside into lush, fertile farmland.

Then imagine that one day, all four of your darling, lively,
lovely children fell ill with raging temperatures. You try waiting
out the fever, but it only gets worse. You and your spouse frantically
do everything you can to save your children—you bathe them in
cool water, you try coaxing liquids down their feverish throats,
you even invoke the help of "spirits." Nothing helps.

Finally night comes and you lie down with your mate to
snatch a tiny bit of rest. You lean over to kiss your loved one's
brow . . . and are startled to find a fever raging there, too.

Desperate, you load your ailing family into your ancient
and dilapidated horse-drawn wagon. You race toward the nearest
town—a good forty miles away—as fast as your horse and your
family can stand.

As morning breaks, you storm into town. You jump down off of the wagon and bellow for a doctor. Soon a sleepy physician staggers out of his bedroom and makes his way toward you. You quickly escort him to your family and describe the sickness.

"Yes, yes, I've seen this illness many times before," the doctor says. "It's responsible for half the graves you see in our cemetery over there. People just kept getting sick; wasn't nothing I could do for 'em."

Your heart sinks.

"And, say—looks like you've got it now," he continues.

You mop your brow. The telltale signs are there, all right. You look at your family. Death seems to hover over the wagon. *How can it end like this?* your spirit screams.

"I never could do nothin' for our people when they got sick like this," you hear the doctor sigh. "So many died."

He shakes his head and quietly rustles the contents of his black bag. You hardly notice that he takes out a syringe loaded with a clear liquid.

"But now . . ." he says.

What? your mind shouts. You snap out of your daze, barely catching the doctor's next words, which sound like *"But now,* with this new drug here, we can save all of 'em. Let's hurry and get their sleeves rolled up. This'll make 'em better in no time."

But now—the two sweetest words in your universe at that moment. Death was inches away. *But now . . .*

That's exactly the mood Paul sets in this passage. He has just told the Colossians that they were diseased, ill, as good as dead in their old life before Christ. Then he comes to verse 22: *"But now* he has reconciled us to himself . . ."

Do you get that? He has reconciled you by Christ's physical body through death to make you holy, without blemish, free from accusation. Our reconciliation to God began with God.

It may be that some of us believe we decided one day "to accept Jesus as our Savior." If we mean by that that one day we committed our lives to Christ, great! But we must not let that terminology move us away from a profound spiritual truth: Our salvation, our reconciliation, does not originate with us. Our salvation originates with God. It is God who has reconciled us to himself. It is not we who do it ourselves.

If we fail to see this we will never understand the grace of God. It was the grace of God that determined we should be reconciled. It was the grace of God that determined how we should be reconciled. It was the grace of God which made the means of reconciliation available to us. It was divine initiative from start to finish.

These people in Colossae—and we today—need to be reminded that believers are what they are because of divine initiative. God, in grace, reconciled them to himself.

Something else of great importance needs to be noticed, too. Verse 22 says, "Now he has reconciled you *by Christ's physical body* through death." The divine incarnation is involved.

Christians must remember that the only reason they can be reconciled to God, have their alienation taken away, their antagonism abolished, their evil activities forgiven, is that God, in Christ, came into the world in the incarnation, assumed our humanity, lived physically among us, and died a physical, horrible death on a cruel cross.

It was necessary to remind the Colossians of this, you remember, because a heresy then current suggested that experience unrelated to the physical death of Christ could lead to fullness of life.

Even today people will try to pry your attention away from Calvary to focus it on any number of self-improvement schemes. Even in the church there is a tremendous emphasis on people's finding fullness of life or enhancing their potential. You find scores of people trying to get their lives "integrated" or "put together" or "reconciled."

Many of these programs so heavily emphasize individual fulfillment that they overlook the death of Christ. We need to remind ourselves that there is salvation in no other; there is no other name under heaven given to men whereby we must be saved. We dare not move into any type of "reconciliation ministry" that ignores the death of Christ. It becomes sub-Christian the moment it does.

The only basis upon which sinful man can be reconciled to God is through the death of Christ. The wages of sin is death. We must pay it ourselves, or allow Christ to pay it for us. His death substitutes for ours. Only through his death on the cross is it possible for us to escape eternal death and everlasting separation from God.

You'll never get right with God by doing an end-run around the cross. You'll never have sins forgiven on any other basis than the death of Christ. Our reconciliation is based on divine initiative, divine incarnation, and divine intervention in the death of Christ. Christ was born in Bethlehem with Calvary in mind. Christmas had Good Friday in view right from the start.

Perhaps one of the best illustrations of this is the famous story of the Prodigal Son. You remember how the father bestowed all kinds of benefits on the son. The son went his own way. He left for a far country and forgot his father. There he wasted his resources on wild living. Looking for self-fulfillment, he finished up in a pigsty, trying to beg some husks off the swine.

One day as he thought about all this, he came to himself and said, "I will arise and go to my father." The father was waiting, ready to receive him to himself. The son is wonderfully reconciled to his father.

In the same way, God the Father has done all that is necessary for anyone to be reconciled to him. God stands at the cross, opens wide his arms, and says, "I've done everything necessary for absolutely everybody to be reconciled to me. You come and be reconciled."

Christians say, "I've done it, I've done it! Once I was far off, but now I have been reconciled to God. Now I'm justified in God's sight."

That's what Paul says in verse 22: "But now he has reconciled you by Christ's physical body through death to present you holy in his sight without blemish and free from accusation."

Paul has in mind a law court in which someone is presented before the judge. The judge hears the evidence, passes sentence, pays the sentence himself, and declares the prisoner free to go. No further charges can be brought against him.

When people alienated from God, antagonistic in attitude, and active in evil are reconciled to God, they are justified by God.

God brings them into his presence and declares them utterly and totally forgiven. No further charges can be brought.

Suppose someone living in a nice, quiet neighborhood commits a horrible crime. Television crews arrive and interview the guilty person's neighbors. The neighbors say things like, "Oh, he's such a nice, quiet man. He walks his dogs and cuts his grass. He's a good neighbor; never gave me any trouble at all. I never bothered him and he never bothered me. I can't believe that anything like this could happen in our neighborhood. I just don't know what to say." I'm sure you've seen many such exhilarating TV interviews.

The perpetrator is then brought into court and found guilty. He's packed off to jail, and twenty years later he's released and goes back to his neighborhood. You'd think that after twenty years the people would have forgotten, wouldn't you? You'd think that after twenty years in jail people would say, "Boy, he's paid his dues. Let's receive the guy back again." But that doesn't happen very often. Often he discovers he's not very welcome in the neighborhood. Guilt is still attached to him.

I've got great news for you. When you are justified by God, you're welcome back in God's neighborhood. He doesn't keep hitting you over the head with what you did. He doesn't keep laying a guilt trip on you. You are justified. You are presented before him holy, without blemish, free from accusation.

A Christian can look back and say, "That's what I was, but this is what I am. I am reconciled. I have been justified. No guilt attaches."

It's a wonderful, wonderful thing to bear in mind where we were.

But it's infinitely more glorious to understand where we are as believers in the Lord Jesus Christ.

The Cross That Liberates

*When you were dead in your sins and in the
uncircumcision of your sinful nature, God made
you alive with Christ. He forgave us all our sins,
having canceled the written code, with its
regulations, that was against us and that stood
opposed to us; he took it away, nailing it to the
cross.*

D o you know any couples who can't seem to stop fighting? They kick, they scratch, they claw, they bite, they argue, they bicker, they insult, they blame, they fume. They dredge up old hurts and fling them in their partner's face.

I wish these couples could see the difference that forgiveness makes in a marriage. I wish they could see the couples who come into my office with grudges as big as elephants and leave with a flicker of old love restored. These restorations don't happen all the time, of course, but once in awhile a couple will try forgiving each other. What a thrill it is for a pastor to see forgiveness bring life and laughter to marriages that once were dead and full of hate.

Forgiveness. What a beautiful word, and how much we all stand in need of it! Not only in our marriages, but wherever people are involved. Without it, life is harsh and bitter and cold and dreadful—in a word, hopeless.

"Hopeless" describes exactly our position prior to the cross. Before the cross, we were bitterly at odds with God. He would reach out in love, and we'd bite and scratch and kick and insult.

Then Calvary came, and God offered us forgiveness in Christ. His forgiveness allowed a real love affair to begin.

Christian, never forget: In Christ we have been forgiven. In verse 14 Paul uses some interesting little pictures to describe it. "Having canceled the written code, with its regulations, that was against us and that stood opposed to us; he took it away, nailing it to the cross." What does this mean?

First, he talks about the code that was canceled. Think of the Ten Commandments. Think of how often you've broken them. Think of the things you've done that you shouldn't have done. Think of all the things that you could have done that you haven't done. Visualize, if you can, God making out your bill and how much in debt you are. Take a good, long, hard look . . . and declare bankruptcy. No way can you pay that bill.

Here is the great, good news: Jesus Christ took the bill, took it to the cross, and stamped right across it, "Paid in Full." That's what forgiveness means. He has canceled the debt. He has paid it in full. You are no longer indebted, you are no longer bankrupt in the courts of heaven. Forgiven! Did you do it? No. It was in Christ that you were forgiven.

Then Paul says something else. He says Christ, having forgiven all our sins and canceled the written code that was against us, took it away, nailing it to the cross.

When somebody was crucified in ancient times, part of the Roman cross was called the *titulus*, from which we get our word *title*. The *titulus* was nailed above the head of the crucified person.

Do you remember the *titulus* that Pilate wrote for Jesus? "This is Jesus, the King of the Jews." Normally, they put on the cross a list of the crimes for which the person was being crucified. That way, when people looked at the cross, they would see the person on it, read the *titulus*, and say, "Boy, he sure deserved it."

When they looked at Christ's cross, all they saw was this strange thing: "This is Jesus of Nazareth, the King of the Jews." That's why the Jews said, "No, no, put on 'he said that he was King of the Jews'!" But Pilate said, "What I have written, I have written."

The Jews wanted him crucified for blasphemy; Christ had claimed to be King of the Jews. Pilate—weak, wet person that he was—still had some bit of backbone in his spaghetti, and told them his version would stand.

The unseen *titulus* on the cross of Christ was a list of my crimes and of yours. The sins of the whole world were written long on that unseen paper.

When Christ went to the cross, in one hand he took the code, the bill of our indebtedness, and wrote "Canceled" across it. With the other hand he took the *titulus*, the explanation of all our sin, and nailed it over his own head.

When people look at the cross and see Jesus hanging there, they don't see Jesus of Nazareth the King of the Jews. They see a record of the sins of people like you and me. He died for us, took our sin, and nailed it to the cross. The cross means that we have been forgiven in Christ.

But it means more than that. The cross means not only that Christ died for us, but that we died with him. It means that I died to all that it was necessary for Christ to die for.

A lot of people have the idea that they can live for all the things Christ died for. Nonsense! When Paul talks about us dying with Christ, he means that we're aware that Christ died for us, and we know we died with him.

He doesn't mean we are dead. He doesn't mean those things are dead. He just means that the relationship has been terminated.

One of the happiest days of my life took place about 40 years ago, and I can still visualize it. I was standing on parade in Portsmouth, Hampshire, England, in my Royal Marine uniform. The officer came on parade and made an announcement which said, in effect, "David Stuart Briscoe, RM128227, you are now temporarily dismissed from His Majesty's Royal Marines and may, if you wish, seek civilian employment. But if you desire to sign on for another seven years, we'll be happy to entertain you."

I desired very much not to sign on for an additional seven years. I was free!

There was a very nice gentleman in the barracks there called the Regimental Sergeant Major. He had an immaculate uniform, a big voice, and a big mouth. He loved to come right behind us while we were on parade, standing stiff as ramrods, staring straight ahead. He would open his cavernous mouth one inch behind our ears and shout at the top of his voice, "Am I hurting you?"

We had to answer, "No, Sergeant Major."

"I can't hear you!"

"No, Sergeant Major."

"You're not moving your head, are you?"

"No, Sergeant Major."

He finished this little routine with a line that explained his belligerent behavior: "I'm standing on your hair at the back!" That meant it was longer than the regulation 1/8 inch. And that was verboten.

"One pace forward! Right turn! March! Right, left, right, left!"

We marched over to the barber's where we got clipped right over the top of the head.

Nice man. We really enjoyed him. Friendly, warm, personable, interested in our well-being.

Don't you believe it! Whenever we saw him coming, our backs would spring up straight. We'd swing our arms up to the shoulder, thumb on top, heels dug in. Remember, these are veterans I'm talking about, not recruits. That's what you did when the RSM showed up.

The day I was released I saw the RSM walking toward me. My head sprang up, my back straightened, I began to march. My arm went to leap up to salute . . . and a little voice inside me said, "You died to him."

And I said, "What?"

"You died to him."

"But he's not dead!"

"That's right, and you're not dead, either."

"Well, if he's not dead, and I'm not dead, how could I have died to him?"

"Simple. You have no further obligation to him, and he has no further authority over you. So if you'd like, you can go on looking silly—marching around like that, swinging your arm up to salute. You'll look very funny, but go right ahead if you want to. Why, though? Why continue in subjection to that to which you died?"

And I thought, *I don't really want to.*

So a very funny thing happened. My back curled ever so slightly, my hands found their way deliciously into my pockets— they had not been there for two long years—I scuffed my heels, and as I walked past the man, I whistled.

He went red, turned to purple, turned to puce. He couldn't do a thing.

That's what the cross means. You died to all that it was necessary for Christ to die for. Why go on living to it? Why be in bondage to it? You don't have to be. You're free! You've been liberated from all the hurtful things that would take your eyes off Christ.

The next time they come your way, just whistle at 'em. They can't do a thing.

Don't Run on Empty

... and you have been given fullness in Christ,
who is the head over every power and authority.

I magine that you have been invited to Thanksgiving dinner at the home of the richest man in the world. You pull up a chair at a table two football fields long that's piled high with so much turkey and dressing and potatoes and bread and carrot cake and pumpkin pie and mixed vegetables and milk and anything else you can think of that the table is about to break under the load. Your host tells you to take your fill of anything you see. In fact, he insists on it.

"Thank you very much," you say. "Might I please have half a cranberry?"

Your astonished friend nearly chokes on a candied yam.

"What?" he exclaims. "My dear guest, look at the table! You'll never get full that way. Please, eat! I've placed all this here just for you!"

"Thank you, you're so kind," you respond. "Maybe I'll take a whole cranberry after all."

"You don't understand," your exasperated host replies. "You have available to you everything you need to get full. You don't have to leave hungry. *Please* take advantage of it. That's why I invited you! You're hungry, and I'm in a position to give you everything you need to be full."

"Thank you so very much," you say. "Perhaps I will have a sip of water with my cranberry."

Your host shakes his head. He's invited the whole town for dinner at different times, and always it's the same. No amount of pleading or cajoling can get his guests to eat anything except parts of cranberries and thimblefuls of water. But he'll keep trying.

Ridiculous, we say. Who would ever act like that? If it were us, we'd gobble up so much food they'd have to use a bulldozer to move us out.

Why is it, then, that when it comes to getting full spiritually, we settle for half a cranberry?

Paul doesn't want that for us, and in this passage he reminds us of an essential key to successful Christian living. "If you're a believer," Paul would tell us, "you have been 'plugged into' Christ's fullness. You have an 'in' to reality. You have the password into all the resources you could ever dream of. You have in Christ all that it takes to be all that you need to be, all that God wants you to be."

Not infrequently you'll come across people who are saying either in word or deed that their lives are impoverished. Sometimes, remarkably, you'll find a believer—related to Christ in whom all fullness dwells—who for some reason is looking for something else. He is not satisfied. She is not filled full.

Remember this: The extent to which you need something else to fill you full is the extent to which you find Christ deficient. If you find Christ deficient, then you have found something in contradiction of Scripture which says, categorically, that in Christ all the fullness of Deity resides in bodily form. So let me say it again: The extent to which you need something else to fill you full is the extent to which you find Christ deficient.

We've got to decide, is it true that in Christ all fullness is to be found? And then, is it true that I am related to him and in him? If so, we discover that in Christ we've got all that it takes.

You'll find in the church today many people propagating all kinds of things that believers "need." Not infrequently these things that Christians "need" have exceedingly tenuous connections to Christ, "in whom all fullness dwells." As soon as someone tells you that you need this and you need that and you need the other, ask yourself, "Is this in any way diverting my attention from Christ? Is there any sense in which this is perverting the gospel of Christ, which tells me all fullness is in him? If I get into this particular thing, will it in any way subvert the authority of Christ in my life?"

Beware! Scripture declares that in Christ is all fullness, and if you are related to him, you have been given all fullness. We don't need something super-added, extra-plus to Christ. What we need to do is to make daily discoveries of all that we already have in him.

Paul goes on to talk about this Christ being the One who is the head over every power and authority. Remember that there were teachers coming into Colossae who suggested that if God were Spirit (which is good) and man was matter (which was evil), the only way in which God and man could relate would be by a series of emanations—all kinds of intermediaries between God and man so that, slowly and insidiously, it would be possible to construct a bridge.

Paul says, in effect, "OK, let's assume that there are all kinds of powers and authorities. Just for the sake of argument, let's assume that there are all kinds of things out there we don't understand. Don't worry about them, because there is one thing you need to know and it is this: Whatever they are and whoever they are, Christ is in control. He is head over every power and authority."

Paul didn't go in for all the magical stuff that many of his contemporaries were into, but he did realize there were supernatural things going on all around him which he couldn't see. He didn't buy into all the elaborate spiritual hierarchies that many pagans talked about, but he did preach about Christians being in a real battle with real evil spirits. He wasn't afraid of them, but neither did he play with them.

Some people ignore any thought of spiritual dynamics in our world. They rush headlong into all kinds of things which may have demonic connections. They scamper impulsively into things which not infrequently are rooted in the occult. Even Christians are so careless today that they play around in these things and don't seem to understand that they are very, very vulnerable when they get there.

We must understand that we are rooted in Christ, and that he is the one in whom all fullness is found. He is in control of those things. If we keep our eyes on him, we'll know victory over whatever powers come against us.

Victory *is* ours in Christ, but we'll only share in that victory if we're full. Half-starved Christians who refuse to feast on Christ's bounty make poor soldiers against the demons of hell.

Why choose half a cranberry when the owner of all the farms in the cosmos invites you to supper? He's offering you the delicacies of heaven without cost or limit.

Why not dig in?

Away with the Old Life!

In him you were also circumcised, in the putting
off of the sinful nature, not with a circumcision
done by the hands of men but with the
circumcision done by Christ, having been buried
with him in baptism and raised with him
through your faith in the power of God, who
raised him from the dead.

Some people think you shouldn't talk about circumcision in polite company. Mention it, and some folks either blush or blanch. I think it's time we talked about it.

Now, don't get worried. There's no need to change your pigmentation. We won't go into its surgical or anatomical details. But we can learn something of great importance from circumcision, so let's talk about it and remember what it's all about.

God's covenant with Abraham directed Abraham and his descendants to be circumcised as the outward and visible sign of an inward and spiritual relationship. Through the prophets God later explained that it wasn't enough to have an outward and visible sign if there wasn't an inward and spiritual reality. Accordingly, the prophets used to talk not just about being circumcised physically, but being circumcised in heart. Godly Israelites needed a spiritual, inner circumcision that matched up to the external symbol.

In the same way, Paul says, Christ has come and worked circumcision in our lives—not the cutting off of part of our flesh, but doing away with the sinful nature, what Paul calls "the body of the flesh."

This expression causes us some problems. When it talks about circumcision or the putting away of the body of the flesh, it is not saying that your physical body is sinful. It's not talking about that part of you that hangs between your bones and your skin and is sometimes hanging over your belt.

When it talks about flesh, it means that bias to sin that's in all of us. All of us have a bias to sin. Christ can circumcise that bias when we come to him.

That doesn't mean God takes away our ability to sin. Rather, he gives us the ability and desire not to sin. Let me repeat that; when it says that Christ circumcises us in the body of the flesh, it doesn't mean that God takes away our ability to sin. What it does mean is that he gives us the desire and the ability not to sin.

We may not utilize that ability; we may stifle that desire and go on with the old life. When that happens we veer off track and end up in all kinds of destructive junk.

Do you have a problem with the old sinful nature in terms of lust? Has it been circumcised? Has it been put off?

Do you have a problem with the old nature in terms of greed? Has it been circumcised? Has it been been put off?

Do you have problems in telling the truth, in desiring righteousness? Well then, you've got a bias to sin there; it must be put off.

In Christ we have been circumcised! Sin has been put off! Learn to live in the reality of it.

But there's even more. Paul says we have been buried with Christ. Verse 12: "Having been buried with him in baptism . . ." He relates baptism to burial, which in turn seems related to circumcision. This is not an easy passage of Scripture.

What does it mean when it says we have been buried with Christ?

Those of you who have attended the burial service of a loved one know its sense of finality, its sense of termination. You stand around the graveside, and as you look into that empty grave you see the casket containing the remains of your loved one. You know that very shortly it will be lowered into the ground and that will mean termination.

Americans do funerals very nicely. They put artificial green grass around and they cover the casket with flowers. Everyone stands around the casket, a few words are said, and everyone leaves. You don't see the coffin lowered into the ground or the dirt heaped around it.

In England it's not so nice as that. There's just an open hole in the ground, ropes are put through hoops on the casket's side, and family members lower the casket into the ground. Then they take soil and begin to cover it. There is an awful sense of termination in burial.

When Paul says you were buried with Christ, he means your conversion terminated the old life. It came to an end. When you identified with Christ, you said goodbye to the old stuff.

Forget this, and there's a good chance you'll slip back into the old ways. You might be crucified with Christ, you might be buried with Christ, in fact, you're dead, but unfortunately you won't lie down. Listen, you need to borrow a shovel.

Paul says you have been buried with him in baptism.

We need to be careful at this point. When it says we are buried with him in baptism, some people have assumed that all you've got to do is be baptized and automatically these spiritual things happen. They want it done as soon as possible to their children. They want to bring infants to church for baptism so that magically, mystically, wonderfully, mechanically, the children get an eternal life insurance policy.

Clearly that's not right. Baptism is never a substitute for faith. Have you got that? Baptism is significant and important, but it's never a substitute for faith.

Some people, hearing this, say, "There you have it. It's obvious, then, that you don't baptize little children. You wait until people have exercised faith and then you baptize them on confession of faith. That way nobody gets confused that baptism substitutes for faith."

That's sound reasoning, but Paul does seem to suggest a link between circumcision and baptism.

Israelites were circumcised on their eighth day of life, before they could exercise any faith at all. Those who see baptism as the New Testament equivalent of circumcision firmly believe that infants of believing parents should be baptized. They see baptism as a sign that the child has entered into the new covenant in the same way that circumcision signified the entrance of an Israelite child into the old covenant. They know that every child must one day come to faith and show the inner reality of the external symbol, but they insist you should not for that reason deny them the outward symbol.

Frankly, I don't care which mode of baptism people use, as long as they don't allow it to become a substitute for personal faith. Baptism is no substitute for personal heart discipleship.

Paul makes this clear in the rest of verse 12 when he insists the key even to baptism is faith: "having been buried with him in baptism and raised with him through your faith . . ." Baptism unrelated to faith is an empty tradition. Baptism as an outward and visible sign of an inward and spiritual grace is profoundly significant.

Let's pull this together. What is Paul saying? He's saying that, one way or another, your baptism is an outward expression of the inward reality of your identification with Christ. You are united to Christ by faith and have died to all that he died to. You've been buried, you've terminated the old life.

Now let me ask something. Is there evidence that in Christ you have been circumcised? Can you say quite frankly that in him you have been buried to the old life and with him you have been raised to newness of life? Can you say that because you have exercised faith in the God who raised Christ from the dead, the power that raised him from the dead is operative in your life and you are alive in him?

Paul says that's what circumcision means. That's what baptism entails.

Whew! We're done with this passage, and I trust nobody's passed out. Wouldn't you agree that circumcision's not really such a hard thing to discuss? It *was* hard to accomplish, however.

It cost Christ his life.

Will the Real Believers Please Stand Up?

*Paul . . . to the holy and faithful brothers
in Christ at Colossae:*

You can learn all kinds of things by reading personal letters. You can glean information about both the sender and the recipient. It seems to me, for example, you could learn at least three things from a letter that began:

My dearest, beloved, adored, treasured, longed-for cupcake,

If you read carefully you will learn that:

1. The author is deeply in love.
2. The recipient is deeply loved.
3. The author is deeply indebted to a cheap thesaurus.

When we read Paul's epistle to the Colossians, we can heartily declare that points (1) and (2) above apply. We have already taken a look at the kind of people Paul was writing to, so perhaps it is appropriate to sum up what we've learned so far. A good place to do that is in Paul's opening lines. While the beginning is always a good place to begin, sometimes it's an equally good place to end. So I hope it turns out in this case.

Five things describe the believers in Colossae. First of all, spiritually they were "in Christ." It would be easy to slide over this phrase if you're not careful, but please do notice that it's a common phrase in this epistle. In fact, it's common in all Paul's writing. He loves the expression.

It's his shorthand term for people who are related to the Lord Jesus. He means that Christ is the atmosphere which they breathe, the dominating factor of their lives, the one who directs them in the way they ought to go.

He also means that when God looks at people who are "in Christ," he doesn't see them in all their failure. He sees them in all the righteousness of the Lord Jesus.

If we were to stand before God in all our uncleanness, we would be unacceptable. But when we're "in Christ," we're clothed with his righteousness and acceptable for his sake.

When Paul writes to people who are "in Christ," he is talking about their spiritual position and condition. At this point we need to ask, "Do I see myself as living 'in Christ'? Do I have a definite union with him? Do I see him as the atmosphere that I breathe, the environment in which I live, the dominating factor of my life? Am I claiming his righteousness when I stand before God, or do I think I'm going to make it on my own?"

These people who are "in Christ" spiritually are also called "holy" from a moral point of view. The word "holy" is a fascinating word. It's a term people react to. It's a word we don't like very much.

Just imagine what would happen if someone were to ask a young person in school, "What is your ambition?" and she were to reply, "I want to be holy." What would be the reaction? The class would crack up. People would think the kid was loony.

Now, why? It's because we don't understand what "holy" means. When people want to make a disparaging remark about somebody, often they'll call him a "holy Joe" or a "holy roller," and the worst thing you can ever be accused of is a "holier than thou" attitude.

Isn't that interesting? It's because we don't like the word "holy." And we don't like it because we don't understand it.

Let me remind you that the root from which we get the word "holy" is the word "to cut."

Ladies, if you are preparing lunch and you use a very sharp knife and cut the end of your finger, the end of your finger becomes separated from the rest of your finger. So "cut" leads to the idea of "separating." "Separating" then leads to the idea of "distinctive," because if the end of your finger is separated from the rest of your finger, it will be very distinctive, indeed. When it becomes distinctive, it will be other than the rest of you. It will be something apart, something else.

That's what "holy" means. Holy means distinctive, separate, other, something else. When God picks out a word to describe himself he uses the word "holy." That means he's distinct. He's separate. He's other. If we can use the colloquial expression, "he's something else."

When we read about people who are "in Christ" spiritually, we must see that they are required to be holy, morally, which means that they live "something else." They live distinctively.

There are some things that "holy" people won't get into. They're too smart to get into them. They won't get into destructive habits because they have a new set of priorities.

Holiness, however, shouldn't only be seen in negative terms. The basic idea of holiness is not negative, it's positive. If we are holy, we live attractive, winsome, definite, distinctive lives. People notice.

Third, the believers in Colossae are described intellectually as "believing." The NIV says "to the holy and *faithful* brothers in Christ," but the word translated "faithful" can equally be translated "believing." "Faithful" and "full of faith" come from the same Greek word—they have only one word for both. If you are full of faith, that is, believing, you should demonstrate it by being faithful. Or put it this way. If you are trusting, you demonstrate it by being trustworthy. The two things always work hand in glove.

These believers in Colossae had intellectually subscribed to the gospel, but it had more than intellectual ramifications. Morally it shaped their lifestyle and spiritually it placed them into Christ. So when we talk about believers, we're talking about people who are spiritually "in Christ," who morally are holy, and intellectually are believing in the truth of the gospel.

But then notice that Paul calls them "brothers in Christ at Colossae." This means there were some sociological differences, too. They had become brothers in Christ. This little group of people that we call the church at Colossae—and it was a little group, not a great crowd like many of our churches today, where you need to hold three services each Sunday except for Easter when you need four—this relatively small group of people regarded each other as brothers.

Many of them, no doubt, had run into real problems with their blood relatives. There'd been some real divisions when they became Christians. Some of you reading this can sympathize with them. When you became Christians, the members of your families didn't like it. They don't like what's happened to you. They resist what you're saying and almost seem to resent what you stand for. But then God steps in, and in one sense, compensates. You can't totally compensate for the estrangement of your blood relatives, but there is some compensation in discovering in the fellowship of believers a whole new set of brothers and sisters.

You are part of a new family—and incidentally, it's a much bigger family. That's one reason people come to Christ in our society. With the breakup of marriage and the family, there are many lovely, lonely, discouraged, disconsolate people. But when they're introduced to Christ and they become a distinctive, spiritual, and believing people, they're introduced to a whole new community. In that new community they find a whole lot of new brothers and sisters.

This is a very full description of a believer. But note that this description is essentially practical. For while Paul talks about them spiritually, morally, intellectually, and sociologically, he also talks about them being geographically in Colossae. In other words, he isn't just sitting in an ivory tower dreaming up some theological thoughts which he floats out into the ether, hoping someone might latch on to them. No, he is sitting in a smelly cell, with a specific town in mind. He knows the people of that town and what they're up against, and he's interested in their becoming spiritually and morally and intellectually and sociologically distinctive believers in Colossae.

Colossae had a great history, but had fallen on hard times. It had been a superior city, but now was being overshadowed by Laodicea and Hierapolis nearby, and Ephesus not many miles away. It was known for its paganism, a place overrun by idolatry.

The apostle says it's there—in that town that had a great history but now had fallen on hard times, in this one-horse town with a chip on its shoulder, in this place riddled with idolatry and governed by paganism—it's in that environment that specific believers were called to live holy, distinctive, winsomely attractive lives.

How does all this apply to us? Very simply. Instead of writing to the holy and faithful brothers in Colossae, the Spirit of God would say to you and me today, "Are you holy, faithful brothers in Christ in your community? In your towns and cities that are riddled with materialism and governed by greed, are you faithful representatives of my Son? The days of the Colossians are long past. It's your turn now. How're you doing?"

If you wrote a truthful letter of reply, what would it say?

Working Out

1. Colossians 2:10-14 mentions at least six things that are true of every believer. These six things are listed underneath this paragraph. Under each item give your own definition of the phrase.

a. Christians have "fullness in Christ."

b. Christians are "circumcised in Christ."

c. Christians are "buried with Christ" in baptism.

d. Christians are "raised with Christ" through faith.

e. Christians are made "alive in Christ."

f. Christians are "forgiven" all their sins.

Now go at this negatively. Suppose you weren't a Christian—what then? Take these same six items, turn them around, and in your own words describe what your life would be like.

a. Non-Christians have "emptiness outside of Christ."

b. Non-Christians are "uncircumcised outside of Christ."

c. Non-Christians are "buried alone" even if baptized.

d. Non-Christians "remain buried" through unbelief.

e. Non-Christians are "dead outside of Christ."

f. Non-Christians are "guilty and responsible" for all their sins.

What action, if any, do these lists suggest you should take in your life?

Second Wind

1. Romans 5:1-11
   What things should believers "rejoice" in? How do you rejoice in them?

2. Ephesians 1:3-14
   What blessings have believers been given through Christ?

3. 1 Thessalonians 4:1-10
   How does Paul connect "doctrine" with "living" in this passage?

4. 1 Peter 1:14-25
   How does Peter say people become "holy" and "pure"?

5. 1 John 5:1-5
   How can you tell if someone is a believer, according to John?

Where Am I Heading?

But now he has reconciled you by Christ's physical body
through death to present you holy in his sight,
without blemish and free from accusation—
if you continue in your faith, established and firm,
not moved from the hope held out in the gospel.
Colossians 1:22-23a

So then, just as you received Christ Jesus as Lord,
continue to live in him, rooted and built up in him,
strengthened in the faith as you were taught,
and overflowing with thankfulness.
Colossians 2:6-7

. . . being strengthened with all power
according to his glorious might
so that you may have great endurance and patience,
and joyfully giving thanks to the Father,
who has qualified you to share in the inheritance
of the saints in the kingdom of light.
Colossians 1:11-12

When Christ, who is your life, appears,
then you also will appear with him in glory.
Put to death, therefore,
whatever belongs to your earthly nature:
sexual immorality, impurity, lust, evil desires and greed,
which is idolatry.
Because of these, the wrath of God is coming.
Colossians 3:4-6

We proclaim him,
admonishing and teaching everyone with all wisdom,
so that we may present everyone perfect in Christ.
To this end I labor, struggling with all his energy,
which so powerfully works in me.
Colossians 1:28-29

Hang in There!

Nobody trains without a purpose.

Aerobics buffs often get up early in the morning to bounce off extra pounds. Their goal is to get in shape.

Weight lifters spend hours in the gym pumping iron and straining muscles to build strength and bulk.

Serious runners log hundreds of miles both on and off the track so that in a key race they don't place 134th out of 135.

They all dedicate themselves to a certain task in order to accomplish a certain objective. They have a goal, a purpose. They give up some things in order to gain better things. They set their sights on an attractive prize and arrange their lives to capture it.

Not everyone who sets out on such a quest finishes well. Legion are the morning aerobicizers who drop out of class to drop in at Dunkin' Donuts. Many are the sore-backed weightlifters who ignore training rules and are forced to abandon the gym. Hundreds are the runners who start a race but never finish.

The Winter Olympics of 1988 enticed millions of viewers to watch the best athletes in the world compete head-to-head. The

U. S. team had few athletes who were expected to do well, but speed skater Dan Jansen was an exception. Hopes were high that he could pick up at least one gold medal.

Those hopes were dashed when Dan fell during competition—not once, but twice. He failed to finish either of the two races he began.

I never heard an explanation for his falls. Was it lack of concentration? Poor equipment? Flaws in the ice? Over-anxiousness? Whatever the reason, the fact is that a highly gifted athlete came away from Calgary bitterly disappointed. He started well, but came away empty.

I'm hoping you who read this book have started out well in the Christian faith. I hope you've got solidly in mind the basics that will carry you through whatever hardships you may encounter in your spiritual walk. You've begun a fantastic journey that leads to unimaginable glory . . . but to reach that goal you've got to stay in the race.

That's what Paul talked about in Colossians 1:23, a verse that begins with an ominous little word—"if." Such a little word, but one that causes great consternation.

To get the full impact of the verse, we need to return to verse 22: "But now he has reconciled you by Christ's physical body through death to present you holy in his sight, without blemish and free from accusation, *if*"—if what?—"*if* you continue in your faith, established and firm, not moved from the hope held out in the gospel."

Paul is talking here about what's often called "the perseverance of the saints." He wants us to understand that those who are reconciled and those who are justified are those who will continue in the faith.

How can you tell if a person is justified? How can you tell if a person is reconciled? How, in other words, can you tell if a person is a real Christian?

All kinds of tests are often given. Sometimes someone will say, "I know he's a real Christian because I remember that ten years ago when a certain evangelist came to town, he went forward when the invitation was given. He got up out of his seat and walked to the front. It's true that we haven't seen hide nor hair of him since that time—he's shown no interest whatever, in fact—

but I clearly remember him getting up out of his seat and walking to the front."

Others might say, "Well, I know she's a Christian because when she was a child she was presented in church for baptism or dedication (I can't remember which), and that's that. She hasn't shown any real interest since then, but she must be a Christian. Clearly she's not a pagan. She was introduced into the fellowship of believers."

Hold on a minute! Paul said that those who are justified and those who are reconciled—truly justified, truly reconciled—*persevere* in the faith. They continue in the faith. They are well-founded, like a solid building on good foundations. They are not easily moved away. They are loyal to the faith. They finish their race.

They have their eyes fixed on the end of their faith, on the hope that is in the gospel. They have an objective to reach, and they dedicate themselves to reaching it. They are utterly convinced of the faith, confident in it. They keep on keeping on.

They didn't make a snap decision about following God and then forget him. They didn't say, "Sure, I'm a Christian," and then go on living in the old way, uninterested in living Christianly.

Those who are truly justified and truly reconciled persevere in the faith. They continue. They're founded. They're rooted, loyal, confident, convinced, growing, and progressing. How much we need to encourage one another in understanding this point!

F. F. Bruce, a British theologian, said, "Continuance [in the faith] is the test of reality."

How do you match up? Can you look back and say, "Because of all that Christ did on the cross, and because I placed my faith in his finished work, I have been reconciled to God. I have been justified and I am determined, by God's grace, to continue in the faith. I'm thankful, and I intend to demonstrate my thankfulness by continuing to follow Christ"?

Christian brother or sister, the gospel's promise is too great and its prize too precious for you to drop out of the race now. Paul himself—no stranger to suffering and ridicule and heartache—wrote, "I consider that our present sufferings are not worth comparing with the glory that will be revealed in us" (Romans 8:18).

Where Am I Heading?

So hang in there! Continue what you started! By doing so, you not only prove the reality of your faith, but guarantee for yourself a prize and treasure and trophy that no shelf on earth could possibly hold up.

Bloom Where You're Planted

So then, just as you received Christ Jesus as Lord,
continue to live in him, rooted and built up in
him, strengthened in the faith as you were taught,
and overflowing with thankfulness.

Sometimes the Milwaukee Bucks of the National Basketball Association frustrate me. They'll start out a game with a rush, really be into the flow of their game, and build a big lead. They find themselves up by twenty points, and then somebody, somewhere, suggests they "protect the lead."

You know what happens. They change tactics, deviating from the way they began, and soon they're in deep, deep trouble. It's frustrating.

I should hasten to add that the Bucks aren't the only ones liable to this sort of thing. Watch any athletic team for very long and most will fall into it sooner or later.

The sad thing is, we Christians sometimes fare no better. We're prone to falling into the same trap.

We trust Christ to be our Lord and Savior, we're running well, and somewhere along the way we change tactics. We forget how we began. And then we're in trouble.

Paul encourages believers to continue in their walk with the Lord in the manner in which they began. To do that, you've got to be clear how you started. How did you start in your spiritual life?

Paul puts it this way: "You received Christ Jesus as Lord." That's how you started. When we talk about receiving Christ Jesus as Lord in our modern setting, we often think in terms of giving people a presentation and then asking them if they'd like to receive Christ Jesus. "Would you like to ask Jesus Christ into your heart?" we ask.

Too often the information is not full at all. The concern is to get people to respond to the information they have been given.

I suspect that when Paul talks about receiving Christ Jesus as Lord, he expected that those he was evangelizing had first of all to receive the truth of Christ. They were utterly pagan before then, and it was entirely necessary to explain Christ. Paul had to explain Christ's pre-incarnate existence, his incarnation, his life, his death, his burial, his resurrection, his ascension, his exaltation, his return in glory. It was necessary to explain these things so that people could begin to understand sin and redemption and justification.

When you look at how Paul writes to new believers, you cannot escape one thing: New believers in Paul's day were well taught in Christian theology.

I don't think it's right simply to say, "To receive Christ Jesus the Lord, you simply open your heart to him. You needn't open your mind to the truth."

The apostle uses the phrase, "you have learned Christ." I submit that you cannot realistically receive Christ until you have learned Christ, until you understand who he is and what he is about.

I'm not suggesting for a minute that you need a Master of Divinity degree before you can be saved. I am saying that receiving Christ means you are intellectually satisfied of the truth concerning Christ.

But notice something else. He says that they received Christ Jesus *as Lord*. Here's another problem in our contemporary evangelism. Not infrequently you'll hear people say things like, "I received Jesus as my Savior at such-and-such a time, but it wasn't until x-number of years later that I received him as my Lord."

I understand what people mean by that. They mean that they started off on their pilgrimage and only later had a deeper experience. I don't have any problems with that. But I do have problems with their terminology.

I don't know how you can receive Jesus without receiving Jesus Christ the Lord. You cannot separate them. Paul is crystal clear at this point. "You received Christ Jesus as Lord."

Look at it this way. You want Jesus to be your Savior, right?

"Yes."

What do you want him to save you from?

"Well, I want him to save me from death. I want him to save me from hell. I want him to save me from the devil."

Good, that's great! Here's a question for you. How can he save you from death and hell and the devil if he hasn't conquered death and hell and the devil? He can't save you from what he hasn't mastered. But if he has mastered these things in order to save you from them, it's simply because he is Lord of these things. Therefore, the idea of him saving you presupposes his lordship.

If the one I am receiving intellectually, emotionally, and volitionally into my life is the Lord, and I recognize that it is only his Lordship that qualifies him to be my Savior, how do you think I can possibly receive him into my life without acknowledging his mastery of my life? I can't.

I'm not saying you have to understand all the ramifications of Lordship or that you've got to be "totally surrendered" (whatever that is). I am saying that people who quite casually bow their heads and say a little prayer without any deeper understanding of Christ or any readiness to submit their lives to him are people who have not adequately seen Christ Jesus as Lord.

Once we have adequately seen him and have begun to live for him, we're encouraged to continue in the way we began. Notice how Paul said it: ". . . just as you received Christ Jesus as Lord, continue to live in him." The word translated "live" here is really the word "walk." I start out by acknowledging his mastery. I acknowledge his rule one step at a time.

When that happens, I begin to bloom where I'm planted. Notice verse seven: "Continue to live in him, rooted and built up in him." You were rooted, you were planted in him. Now continue to be built up in him.

Some people say Paul mixed his metaphors here. Do you know what a mixed metaphor is? It's when you get two ideas in juxtaposition that have no real relationship. A classic example was the British parliamentarian who one day, suspecting something wasn't quite right, stood up and said, "I smell a rat. I see it floating in the air, and I'll nip it in the bud." That's a mixed metaphor.

Paul may be mixing his metaphors, but the idea is obvious. He warns us to make absolutely certain we are rooted in Christ, then bloom where we're planted.

Do you know of anyone who needs a little watering? Can you think of anybody?

"Oh, I've got them rooted, but I'm not too sure they're blooming," you say. "Sure we've got them planted, but they look kind of withered." Listen, they need a ministry of encouragement.

Or is that you?

"Maybe that's what's wrong with me," you say. "I remember getting planted, and I remember receiving Christ, but I guess I didn't continue as I started. I guess I didn't bloom where I was planted."

Be encouraged. Press on!

You do that by developing as you are instructed. That's what Paul says next: ". . . strengthened in the faith as you were taught."

If you started out being taught Christ Jesus as Lord, don't deviate from that. It's basically all you need to know. All kinds of people will come with all sorts of other stuff, but don't move one inch from the fundamental truth that you were taught Christ Jesus as Lord. You received Christ Jesus as Lord. You are rooted in Christ Jesus as Lord. Now continue as you started. Bloom where you're planted. Be strengthened as you were taught, and discover more and more of what's involved in all this.

Finally, Paul says, "Make sure you are overflowing with thanksgiving." The theme here is very simple. It's the picture of a river overflowing its banks.

I submit that when you go deep in Christ, and when you get involved in a group that encourages you, and when you start encouraging others, you'll have so much to be thankful for that your banks will overflow. When your banks overflow you'll find people gathering around those banks to be encouraged themselves. You'll bloom together, and all of you *en masse* can cross the finish line and take hold of the prize held out in the gospel.

Now, how's that for a mixed metaphor?

Power to Persevere

*Being strengthened with all power according to
his glorious might so that you may have great
endurance and patience, and joyfully giving
thanks to the Father, who has qualified you to
share in the inheritance of the saints in the
kingdom of light.*

We Christians aim at such an extraordinary goal that if we couldn't count on some help to reach it, we'd have no hope of succeeding.

I've got great news! Not only can we count on "some help," Paul says we have available to us the very strength that birthed the stars and flung them out into the galaxies.

How great is this power available to us?

Notice that it is not spoken of in accordance with your need. It is not described according to your desire. God's power is described "according to his glorious might."

If God's power were only as great as your need, what a puny God he would turn out to be! If God's might and strength were only as great as your imagination, what a desperately limited God he would be! No, the power and strength of God available to the believer is not according to human need or imagination, but in direct accordance with his majesty and glory.

You have no doubt seen the emergence of several tiny nations in the past few years. You know how to tell when they've come into existence, don't you? First, they've got an unpronounceable name. Second, they have an ambassador to the United Nations. Third, they've got an airline they can't afford.

They have great ideas of majesty and tremendous notions of pomp. They also have a disaster area for an economy, an army that will fit into one jeep (that won't start), and oversized aspirations for glory and grandeur.

How distant that is from our God! God has aspirations of majesty and the power to go with it. He'll strengthen you with that power!

Just imagine what it would be like to say to yourself, "I have decided that my overriding purpose in life is to be worthy of Christ and to remember whom I represent. I'm going to be as committed as I know how to be to please him at all times. I will do this by a life that practically demonstrates what God is doing within me. I will progressively discover more of him, and I will reach my goal because of all his mighty power, the power commensurate with his glory and his majesty."

Just imagine how that would challenge your life! The picture of fulfillment it promises is simply staggering.

Notice, however, that this power is not there so that you will be enabled to do great signs and wonders and all kinds of fabulous, amazing, spectacular things so that people say, "Wow! That's power!"

No, it's amazingly down-to-earth. We are strengthened with all power according to his glorious might so that we might have endurance and patience. You can't get more practical than that.

The power of God is made available to people in superlative measure in order that they might live purposefully and powerfully down here in the normal circumstances of life. Endurance means God's power enables me to respond properly to my external circumstances. Endurance means you've got the strength to finish the race and win the prize.

Are external pressures so heavy upon you that you'd like to bury your head in the sand? Are you captivated by an inordinate desire to head for the bushes, escape to the mountains, to get away from it all?

That's the normal approach, but it's not the one of a person discovering fulfillment. The person discovering fulfillment is in touch with the power of God, a power that equips him to endure the difficult circumstances of life. What a tragedy to see people trying to find fulfillment by running away from their circumstances!

Peter Wilkes tells the story of some London merchants who at the time of the Great Plague in London decided to escape to Manchester to save themselves. What they didn't know was that they carried the plague with them in their clothes. The plague arrived in Manchester when they did.

Escapism, hedonism, and materialism are stuff of which the modern search for fulfillment is made. God says, "Uh-uh. Don't try to escape your circumstances. Live in your circumstances with endurance, strengthened with all my power."

If you're to live in your circumstances, you'll also need patience. Patience is the power to restrain yourself. It's the ability to handle not the external circumstances, but those things that boil up within you. Patience allows you to control lust, greed, inordinate desire, anger, wrath, maliciousness, jealousy, all the things that erupt because we're looking for fulfillment in the wrong place.

We look for fulfillment and can't get it, so we lust for it. We're greedy for it, we're anxious about it. We're angry because we don't have it. We're malicious because other people have it. We're jealous because they have it and we don't. We want it!

God says, "Hey, listen, hold it! You can be strengthened according to the might of my glory so that you'll have endurance to cope with your external circumstances and the patience to deal with your inner passions!"

When that kind of power is in your life, you begin to discover fulfillment. It's true! It really is.

Notice, however, that Paul doesn't talk just about the power of endurance and the power of patience. If he'd done that, he'd have sounded just like a Stoic philosopher. There are plenty of Stoics around. Stoics believe that you should endure everything and be patient about everything, that you should grit your teeth and bear it.

103

I always think of a Stoic when I see Robert Parrish play for the Boston Celtics. They call him "The Chief." My, what a handsome man he is. He stands about seven feet tall, with finely chiseled features, his face betraying no emotion whatsoever. You could never tell if they were on top of the league or at the bottom, if they'd been blown out by thirty points or if they're winning by a mile. You could never tell if he'd just lost his best friend or if he'd just gotten married.

He's a born Stoic. I'll bet he can endure. I'll bet he's patient.

But on the court he looks miserable.

Paul says that when you are strengthened with God's might, you will have great endurance and patience—but joyfully, joyfully! Listen to him: ". . . being strengthened with all power according to his glorious might so that you may have great endurance and patience, and *joyfully* giving thanks to the Father, who has qualified you to share in the inheritance of the saints in the kingdom of light."

That's the difference between striving for the prize of the gospel and straining for a temporal one. You can win an earthly marathon with a grimace on your face and wind up with nothing more than a faded bauble to put on your mantle. But you win the race of the gospel with a smile on your lips and joy in your heart, for you know that you've been qualified to receive the eternal reward of a limitless inheritance.

And you know the best thing of all? In the Christian race, God himself hands out the medals.

To Be or Not to Be

*When Christ, who is your life, appears, then you
also will appear with him in glory. Put to death,
therefore, whatever belongs to your earthly
nature: sexual immorality, impurity, lust, evil
desires and greed, which is idolatry. Because of
these, the wrath of God is coming.*

One of the most famous things that Paul ever said
challenged me as a teen-ager. It became so power-
ful in my thinking that I never got away from it. I had no desire
to. This is what he said: "For to me to live is Christ, and to die is
gain." Think of that!

Do you remember the great Shakespearean drama where
the Prince of Denmark is walking around the battlements of his
castle, looking across to Sweden, and says, "To be or not to be,
that is the question"? Life was so unbearable for him that he was
thinking of ending it, but the thought of ending it was even more
unbearable. He couldn't be or not be, because both were unbearable.

The apostle, I think, could have said the same thing: "To
be or not to be, that is the question." He would have meant just
the opposite of what Hamlet did, however. "If I go on being," I can
hear him say, "Christ is my life, and in him I discover all that I
need for any eventuality. Of course, there are some rather nasty
eventualities. I've been thrown in prison, beaten up, bitten by
snakes, maltreated, stoned. But so what? Christ is my life in all
these things. For to me to live is Christ, and to die is gain."

Why would dying be a gain? Because he enjoyed Christ down here even with stonings and snake bites. When he·died and went to heaven he would enjoy Christ *minus* stonings and snake bites. The key here or there was that Christ was his life. Other things were incidentals.

You know, there are some people whose lives are governed by stonings and snake bites, and there are others whose lives are governed with Christ, who is their life. If we think like the second group, we'll be excited to hear that "When Christ, who is your life, appears, then you also will appear with him in glory."

The Risen Christ, ascended to the Father's right hand, will come in glorious majesty. What a turning point in history that will be!

Some think history simply lurches from one event to another. They look at events and see no rhyme nor reason to them. They see history as one tragedy heaped upon another, believe everything is a mess and a disaster, and wonder what on earth will happen next.

Others see history as moving in cycles. They say that if we just hang in there, we'll come around the corner eventually.

Still others see history moving relentlessly toward God's fore-ordained conclusion.

What is your approach to history? Is it cyclical? Is it one disaster lurching after another? Is it a relentless march toward God's fore-ordained finale?

I know what mine is: It is that Christ, seated at the Father's right hand, is life, and one day when God says, "Enough is enough," he will blow the whistle three times, say "Time's up!" and "Go get 'em!" and Jesus Christ will appear in full glory to be hailed as King of kings and Lord of lords. Those who are Christ's will appear with him, glorified, and will share in his glory.

That's where history is going, folks, and it's either true or it's untrue. Now that's the truth.

But Paul isn't quite finished. Because of all the wickedness mentioned in verse 5, verse 6 will happen. Because of sin, the wrath of God is coming.

We get a little mealy-mouthed about this aspect of Christian truth. It's true that God is a God of infinite love, of infinite grace and mercy. It's also true he's a God of infinite holiness and purity. That means he must reward what is right and punish what is wrong. The wrath of God *is* coming. Christ is our life, he will appear in glory, and he will execute the wrath of God.

What does Christ's coming mean to me? It means that I need to identify those areas in my life which violate what I profess. If Christ is my life, how can I be dominated by anything else? If Christ is my life, how can he become peripheral? If Christ is my life, why do all kinds of opinions and movements and trends make more of an impact on me than what Christ has said? Why do they move me more than what Christ has promised? How do they obscure the fact that eternity is reality and heaven is my home, or that Christ will return in glory, or that the wrath of God is coming? How did I get so fouled up?

When I start thinking it through, I realize I need to apply and obey this truth. Look carefully at what Paul says in verse 5: "Put to death therefore whatever belongs to your earthly nature: sexual immorality, impurity, lust, evil desires and greed, which is idolatry."

Three words leap out: *immorality, impurity,* and *idolatry.* These three must be dealt with by God's people, and the treatment must be radical. Put them to death.

Some researchers estimate that fifty percent of American women commit adultery. Seventy percent of American men commit adultery. You could say we are an adulterous generation.

God calls adultery sexual immorality, and he says it is totally incompatible with Christian profession. It is totally inappropriate and thoroughly and wholly unacceptable, and if you are into it—and chances are that I am addressing people even at this moment who are sitting comfortably in an easy chair, planning to commit adultery before the next chapter—I warn you to cut it out! Put it to death! It is totally unacceptable.

Why? Because Christ is your life, you are bound up with him, and you are planning to appear with him in glory. When he comes in glory, he will judge everyone who does these things. How do you think you can do them and be forgiven when the other guy will be judged?

Impurity and idolatry are just as unacceptable as immorality. You say, "Now, Stuart, calm down. You're getting all worked up. You've no doubt had a week off and you're overdoing it. I mean, you're not going to accuse us of idolatry now, are you? You don't really think we've got little statues carved out of wood to which we bow down and offer bowls of rice?"

No, I don't. Listen carefully to what Paul says—idolatry is much more than that. "Put to death, therefore, whatever belongs to your earthly nature: sexual immorality, impurity, lust, evil desires, and greed, which is idolatry."

Why is greed idolatry? Because whatever I am absorbed with, whatever demands most of my time begins to rule my life. Anything that takes God's place in my life is an idol. "The dearest idol I have known, whatever that idol be, help me to tear it from thy throne, and worship only thee," said the old chorus.

This is radical truth! "If there is an adulterous relationship in your life," Paul would say, "stop it! If your life is becoming obsessed and absorbed by the inappropriate or the unacceptable, make some dramatic, radical changes. Your life depends upon it!"

When Christ, who is your life, appears, then you also will appear with him in glory. That is where your life is heading. That is what you have to look forward to.

Make sure that when that day arrives, it will be a day of rejoicing and glad shouting, and not a day of shame and tears.

That Will Be Perfect!

We proclaim him, admonishing and teaching
everyone with all wisdom, so that we may present
everyone perfect in Christ. To this end I labor,
struggling with all his energy, which so
powerfully works in me.

The awards ceremony at the Olympic Games must be one of the most moving experiences in all the world of sports. Three athletes stand on elevated platforms, ready to receive medals of gold or silver or bronze.

Out of the scores of competitors who began an event, only three are left. They take their places on the platforms, the gold medalist on the highest one of all. They bend down as a judge graces their necks with an award to be cherished a lifetime. Tears stream down their faces as their country's flag is raised and their beloved national anthem rings out. Tears also stream down the cheeks of family, of friends, of countrymen.

Victory is sweet!

All the hours and sweat and pain and sacrifices of the last few years of hard training suddenly seem worth it. They had set their eyes on a goal, and today they attained it. We see their radiant faces shining on our television screens, and we salute them.

Do **you** realize there is a victory stand for believers in Christ Jesus? **Did** you know that right now, at this moment, you are training for the biggest awards ceremony in history? Our pursuit of the Christian walk is heading somewhere, and it's heading somewhere fantastic.

Christian friend, there is an end to our faith. There's an objective to it. When we come to Christ, it isn't just that we look in the past and say, "I feel good about myself." We must look to the future and say, "Where on earth is all this going?"

There is an end, an objective. There is a consummation of our faith. And we must live in the light of it at all times.

Notice that in verse 23 Paul talks about "the hope of the gospel." Notice that in verse 27 he talks about "the hope of glory." That word "hope" is the dominant theme of the Christian gospel, and "gospel," you recall, means "good news." I submit to you that there's no good news if there's no hope. Hope is something that people in all generations and all cultures look for.

The question is, what is the world coming to? What's going to happen to me? Is there any hope?

"Yes!" the Scripture shouts. Tremendous hope is locked up in the gospel for every believer. It is the hope of glory.

The hope of glory means that we have confidence that when we die, we will be raised to newness of life as a result of Christ's resurrection. We will see God in all his glory.

The hope of glory means that those of us who have been reconciled and justified will not only see God's glory, we will share it.

Question: Where is my faith heading? What is the end of my faith?

Answer: The end of my faith is that I will see the glory of God and share in it for all eternity.

When I'm dead, I'm not done with. When I'm dead, I will die in Christ and be raised in him and share in his glory. That's the hope of the gospel. That is the hope of glory.

Paul also talks about the promise of perfection. He says the day is coming when we will actually be presented holy and blameless and faultless, perfect in God's sight.

There is a sense in which we are justified to that position right now. But on that day it will become active and plain and actual. Always remember that Scripture talks about our position *and* about the practicality of our position.

When I joined the Royal Marines they gave me a uniform, but for months they wouldn't let me wear it. That upset me terribly. The only reason I joined the marines was so that I could wear the uniform.

The problem was that although positionally I was a marine—if I had sneaked away I would have been AWOL and they'd have dragged me back and thrown me in the brig—they wouldn't let me out in that uniform until I had learned, practically, how to behave in a manner commensurate with my position.

It is exactly the same way with my justification. As a Christian, I am as justified now as I ever will be. I'm as holy and blameless and without accusation in God's sight as I'll ever be.

But practically I'm not holy. Practically I'm not blameless. Practically you could bring all kinds of accusations against me. (And many of you do. Some of them are justified and some of you have a problem. But we won't go into that now.)

The point is that although we are positionally justified, a day is coming when we will be perfected practically. We will stand before God without a hint or trace of anything of which we could be accused. Nothing will blemish us. We'll be absolutely perfect in his sight.

That's where we're heading, folks. Would you like to know when it will all happen?

It will happen when Christ appears. The Greek word for his appearing is *parousia*. At the *parousia*, we will appear with Christ in glory. That's when we'll be perfect.

But here's the big thing. If we know that's where we're going, and if we know where we are, we will want to be progressing in our practical experience of Christ. Practically we will want to progress so there are fewer and fewer things of which we may be accused. Practically we will want to grow in grace.

As you look back at your life, can you say to yourself, "That's where I was"? As you look at your life today, can you say,

Where Am I Heading?

"That's where I am"? Now can you look ahead and say, "That's where I'm going"?

We must live in the light of where we were, grateful that we're no longer there. We must continue in the light of where we are, concerned that we're still not what we ought to be. And we must press on to know Christ more fully, assured that one day we will stand before God clothed in perfect holiness.

That is where our faith is leading. It's a trip that promises great reward.

Make sure you're along for the awards ceremony!

Working Out

Colossians 1:28-29

1. The word translated "perfect" in Colossians 1:28 comes from the Greek word *teleios*, which means "having attained the end or purpose," "complete," "mature," "perfect." The same word is used in Philippians 3, where Paul says, "I press on toward the goal to win the prize for which God has called me heavenward in Christ Jesus. All of us who are *mature* should take such a view of things. And if on some point you think differently, that too God will make clear to you. Only let us live up to what we have already attained" (Philippians 3:14-16).

A. In Colossians Paul says he wants to "present" every believer perfect in Christ, while in Philippians he says he is talking to those who already are "mature." This means he cannot be talking about people who are without fault or sin. In what sense, then, do you think he means they are "mature"?

B. How does Paul suggest that people get to this stage of maturity? (Look especially at Colossians 1:28b).

2. In Colossians 1:29 Paul says "I labor, struggling with all his energy, which so powerfully works in me." The word translated "struggling" is the Greek word from which we get the term "agony."

A. Notice all the action words in this verse: "labor," "struggling," "energy," "powerfully," "works." What does this imply about the process of becoming "mature in Christ"? Is it an easy process? Does it come by osmosis?

B. In the very next verse (2:1), Paul tells the Colossians that he wanted them to know how much he was struggling for them. Why do you think he wanted them to know? Would that have been an encouragement to them, or a discouragement? Now think of some fellow believers in Christ with whom you work or fellowship. Could you do the same thing for them that Paul did for the Colossians? If so, how? When?

3. Notice in Colossians 1:28 that Paul doesn't say "*I* proclaim him . . . that *I* may present everyone," but that "*We* proclaim him . . . that *we* may present everyone perfect in Christ." But he does say (v. 29), "To this end *I* labor . . ." Why the change in pronouns? Is this significant? How?

Second Wind

1. 1 Corinthians 9:24-27
   How does Paul compare the Christian life with athletics? How do their respective prizes compare?

2. 2 Timothy 4:6-8
   How did Paul characterize his life as he was about to die? To what great encouragement did he look forward?

3. 2 Thessalonians 1:3-10
   Name five things that will happen on the day the Lord Jesus returns.

4. Hebrews 10:32-39
   To what danger may persecution and suffering expose us? How are we encouraged to persevere?

5. 2 Peter 3:3-15
   How can we be certain the Lord Jesus will really return to earth? Why is it taking him so long?

II
Christian Attitudes

Building a Winning Spirit

How Should I Act?

*. . . we have heard of your faith in Christ Jesus
and of the love you have for all the saints—*
Colossians 1:4

*For this reason, since the day we heard about you,
we have not stopped praying for you
and asking God to fill you with the knowledge of his will
through all spiritual wisdom and understanding.
And we pray this in order that you may live a life
worthy of the Lord and may please him in every way:
bearing fruit in every good work,
growing in the knowledge of God.*
Colossians 1:9,10

*Since, then, you have been raised with Christ,
set your hearts on things above,
where Christ is seated at the right hand of God.
Set your minds on things above, not on earthly things.
For you died,
and your life is now hidden with Christ in God.*
Colossians 3:1-3

*You used to walk in these ways, in the life you once lived.
But now you must rid yourselves of all such things as these:
anger, rage, malice, slander, and filthy language from your lips.
Do not lie to each other,
since you have taken off your old self with its practices
and have put on the new self,
which is being renewed in knowledge
in the image of its Creator.*
Colossians 3:7-10

Wooden Apples and Other Delicacies

Wouldn't it be interesting if, when you became a Christian, God said, "All right. My objective is to get you to heaven, so why don't I take you now?"

One problem with that is that we'd delay becoming Christians as long as possible so we could have as much "fun" down here as we could, then get saved and be wafted off to heaven. Being the kind of people we are, that's how we'd operate.

God, however, decided not to do it that way. He doesn't take people off to heaven the moment they become Christians for one obvious reason. He wants them to live out their Christianity on earth before they get to heaven. Earth is the environment in which Christianity is lived.

Some don't like that. They would love to live on earth and forget that they were Christians, remembering it only when they greet St. Peter. They don't want the struggle of living Christianly in a secular environment.

Yet we must remind ourselves that it is down here, with our two big feet squarely planted in the middle of a secular society, that our Christianity is to be lived. Christians have always had to apply themselves to the culture in which they are planted. It is impossible for us to live divorced from our surrounding culture. Let me give an example.

There was a time in my life when I had to determine how I was going to live as a Christian in wartime Britain. Our culture was quite clearly drawn. It presented a unique set of circumstances which I had to confront.

Later in my life I had to ask myself how a Christian should behave as a Royal Marine, an entirely different culture. Subsequently I moved to the United States of America and found myself in a middle class suburb of Old Milwaukee. I said to myself, "Now here is an entirely different culture. What does it mean to be a Christian here?"

The easy thing would be to conform to the prevailing culture and put our Christianity on the shelf, but we're not free to do that. We have to examine our culture in the light of Christianity, stand firm on Christian principles, and challenge our culture to adapt. That's what it means to be godly.

Godliness has a spiritual dimension that is essentially practical. It produces things. It's down-to-earth, solid. A life of faith must express itself in what it does. It can't just put on a show.

If you were to come to my house, I would offer you some fruit. I have a beautiful carved dish, made of solid wood from the Venezuelan jungle. It's carved in solid, heavy black timber in the shape of a leaf. On it are the brightest, most beautiful apples you ever saw. I would welcome you and bring in my big, heavy, carved plate of apples, and I'd invite you to take one.

I have enormous fun doing that, because for years I've been giving away those apples. The same apples. You see, they're made of the same Venezuelan wood as the dish, and you can't tell it until you try to bite into one. I love watching people come in for counseling and go out with broken teeth. I'm kidding!

You can carve wood to look like fruit, but that's not fruit. Fruit is the natural product of a healthy tree, the external evidence of inward vitality. Spiritual fruit is the natural product of a healthy faith, the external evidence of a vital internal life. The believer's internal life must show itself in external works. Fruitfulness is simply the demonstration of godliness. Our faith motivates us to good works. We do what we do as unto the Lord, and we're rewarded with fulfilled lives.

Do you want fulfillment? That's where it's found, says Scripture.

Unfortunately, people hell-bent on personal satisfaction won't believe it. "You've got to be kidding!" they'll say. "Are you trying to tell me that fullness of life is found in good works prompted by faith? Listen, I've had it up to here with serving, and I've had it up to here with giving, and I've had it up to here with being driven to exhaustion serving God and serving people. I'm going to please myself from now on."

God says, "Go right ahead, just so long as you don't want fulfillment."

The fruitful life leads to fulfillment. The fruitful life progressively makes new discoveries of God and enjoys a new devotion to God. Progress, progress, growth, development.

A sad commentary on the experience of many Christians is that they decide to go so far and no farther. "That's it," they say, and they never progress an inch.

If I ever sense that my discovery of God has ground to a halt, if I ever discover that my devotion to God has reached a plateau, then I can be absolutely certain that my life is being filled with things that will never provide fulfillment.

Do you want to be fulfilled? Then discover for yourself what a life of fruitfulness has to offer.

And stay away from wooden apples!

A Drink That Satisfies

*... we have heard of your faith in Christ Jesus
and of the love you have for all the saints ...*

O ccasionally after one of our church services people will stand in the foyer, look across the crowd, and see a former college classmate. "I don't believe it," they'll gasp. "Look at him. I remember what he used to get into when he ... ha ha ha, hee hee, oh, he's the last person!"

They make their way across the foyer, compare notes, and discover that the other person was thinking exactly the same thing about them. They discover that even though they were into all kinds of junk way back then, somewhere along the line they came to faith in Christ Jesus, their life was changed, and they've become holy and faithful brethren in Christ.

It was like that in Colossae. Everybody knew everyone else's background. Knowing their background, knowing what they'd done, nevertheless there was a genuine, loving concern for one another.

Now, remember that we're talking about a little community here. One of the interesting things about a large church is that you can dodge the people you want to avoid. You can look the other way or maneuver around them or come to a different service or go to a different small group. If somebody upsets you somewhere, you can go someplace else and still be part of the fellowship. The problem with that is that it can make our relationships superficial.

In Colossae they didn't have that freedom. They'd all been reared in Colossae and had probably known each other since they were knee high to a grasshopper. They'd known everything that everybody had got into. There were no secrets. It had a small town mentality, a small town involvement, the gospel had come in, and the most unlikely people had believed.

Their problems were compounded because some of the church's members were Jews and some were Gentiles, some were slaves and some were slave owners, some were men and some were women. Many in these groups detested each other externally, but they learned to love each other in Christ despite their suspicions and animosities.

Why? Because the apostle Paul taught that in Christ all these barriers and sociological chasms had been bridged. They could now begin to live as one body. They began to love each other, and outsiders noticed.

"Something's going on here," they said.

"What's going on," the Christians said, "is that God has worked in our lives and has brought us to faith in Christ, and he's encouraging us and enabling us to love the saints."

The key to this love is found in the very last expression of Colossians 1:8, where Paul talks about their love "in the Spirit."

Let's face it, as a friend of mine used to say, "God must love strange people—he sure made plenty."

No doubt you've heard it said that often it's harder to get along with God's people than it is to get along with pagans. Frankly, I've said it. I've got some pagan friends with whom I never have a wrong word. But with some Christians . . .

The point is that there's every possibility for things going wrong unless the Spirit of God works in our hearts. When we allow the Spirit to work in our hearts, he not only can bring us to faith in Christ, but he can actually bring us to love the saints.

That's what Paul was so grateful for. He could see it happening in the church at Colossae.

If the great apostle were alive today, would he see it happening in our churches? If he showed up at this Sunday's services, would he come away grateful to God for the loving attitudes and actions of the people that he saw there?

Or better yet: If he visited our homes and businesses this week, during the busiest part of the day, would he give thanks for the acts of love he saw Christians bestow upon one another?

Just what would the apostle see?

I saw a letter the other day from one believer to another. The writer, a black, was thanking the recipient, a white, for his help in a proposed project designed to help the evangelical black community. This is part of what it said:

> I had no dream that the depth of your commitment to the project was as great as I learned during our time with you. I labor under no illusion regarding the difficulty facing us in this venture, yet I am overwhelmed with a sense of the presence of God with us and His approval of the "rightness" and timeliness of the project. I welcome and embrace the opportunity as heaven-sent and God-ordained to minister life to our people with your help for His glory.

That's what it's all about! Two people of different race, of unlike culture, of separate geographical location, coming together through Christ in love to address a great need.

When we respond to our Lord's call for Christians to love one another, this old world will get a glorious taste of the delicacies of heaven. The elixir of love is irresistible.

Can thirsty souls get a drink from your cup?

A Walk That Pleases

*... since the day we heard about you, we have
not stopped praying for you and asking God to
fill you with the knowledge of his will through
all spiritual wisdom and understanding. And we
pray this in order that you may live a life worthy
of the Lord and may please him in every way:
bearing fruit in every good work, growing in the
knowledge of God ...*

You've probably heard about the sincere young
Christian who deeply desired to know God's will
for his life. He had some important choices to make and didn't
want to make a mistake.

He decided to use the "pin the tail on the Bible" method
of guidance. Do you know the procedure? You close your eyes, open
your Bible at random, and pin your finger on a verse. (I don't
recommend it.)

The young man prayed: "Lord, show me the way to go." He
shut his eyes, opened his Bible, and pointed.

"And Judas went out and hung himself," the verse said.

This wasn't so good. Perhaps his finger had missed the
right spot? He tried again.

"Go thou, and do likewise," the new verse said.

This was awful. Surely something had gone wrong! The
third time was certain to be the charm. He closed his eyes and
his finger found a new mark.

"And what thou doest, do quickly," it said.

He never used the method again.

A knowledge of God's will is one thing no believer can do without. Paul was convinced that his Colossian friends had to have it.

We must have it, too. When we are filled with that knowledge, spiritual wisdom and understanding are the natural overflow. Let me break this down for you.

Paul is not saying that he wants each of the Colossians to know intellectually what God's will is. You have to start there, but you've got to go much further than that. You have to act on what you know.

But even that is not enough. After you've discovered God's will and have done it, you must come to delight in it. When you do, you'll sense new direction. There'll be a purposefulness about your life—you'll discover what God wants you to be.

I don't mean that you'll know all the minute details of God's will for your life. I'm not so sure God is concerned about all the minute details. I worry when people talk about God's will as if it were a high wire, easy to topple off if you're not careful to keep your balance.

God's will isn't a high wire. God's will is a 12-lane highway. He's got you and me going in a certain direction, and the varieties of possibility are boundless.

To be filled with the full knowledge of God's will doesn't mean you've got to know absolutely everything about everything, that you must know what God wants you to do at every moment in every circumstance. That's not it.

On the other hand, Paul does want us to understand that God has a plan for our lives, a good and acceptable and perfect plan. We discover what it is in general terms from Scripture. When we do what it requires of us, increasingly we'll delight in it.

As a result, we gain a sense of spiritual wisdom—not street smarts, but spiritual wisdom—and a measure of spiritual knowledge. They inform us of the spiritual realities in our lives. We're in tune with heaven, we're in step with the Spirit. Therein, says Paul, is fullness of life.

This provides a challenge.

What happens if I've been totally committed to doing my own thing? What happens if I've already decided what I want to do with my life, and I've been happy doing it?

What happens if suddenly God blows the whistle and says, "Foul!"

What do I do? Start yelling at the umpire? Or do I say, "Okay," and say to myself, "What did I do wrong?" The answer will come loud and clear: "You didn't take time to discover God's will. You weren't interested in doing God's will, therefore you haven't the remotest idea of the sheer delight in doing his will. You've only been interested in doing your own will. You've been happy to do it, and have expected God to smile benignly upon you and bless you out of your socks."

If that's what's wrong, I've got to go back to the drawing board and decide if I'm going to walk with God and be filled with the knowledge of his will. Only when I do that can I enjoy a life of purposefulness. My new, overriding purpose will be "to live a life worthy of the Lord." What does that mean?

The word translated "live a life" is actually the Greek word "walking." The Christian life is frequently described as a walk. It gives the idea of progression and reminds us that the Christian life is one step after another. It's not just one big step. We don't become perfect immediately. But when I know I represent my Lord, when I know that in some way my conduct is tied to the glory of his person, I'll be careful. I don't want my behavior to reflect negatively on him.

Some people take a step into Christ and they stop. They're stuck. You come across them years later, and they haven't gotten anywhere.

Those who are living a life worthy of the Lord are not taking a single step. They're walking in him. They are progressively, situation by situation, circumstance after circumstance, doing and delighting in his will.

The King of England's two sons were in Hyde Park. The Prince of Wales said to the Duke of York, "I bet you a shilling that all fat policemen have bald heads." The Duke said, "You're wrong."

Just then, a fat policeman came along on cue. They didn't know how to dislodge his British policeman's helmet, but fortunately there was a little Cockney kid from the east end of London nearby. They said to him, "I say, old fellow [that's how king's sons tend to speak], do you think you can dislodge that officer of the law's helmet?"

"Yes," he said.

"We'll give you a shilling if you do," they replied.

"I'll do that for nothing," he answered.

He picked up a stone and threw it . . . bulls-eye! Off came the policeman's helmet. Sure enough, the fat policeman had a bald head. The Prince of Wales turned to the Duke of York and said, "You owe me a shilling."

They were settling their debts and their winnings when the portly officer descended upon them, grabbed the boys, and in typical police fashion, got out his little notebook, licked his pencil, and said, "What's your names?"

"Prince of Wales," said the first boy.

"First you assault my person, then you insult my uniform!" the officer snarled. "I could have you on charges for this. What's your name?"

"I really *am* the Prince of Wales," came the reply.

"I don't believe you. What's your name, then?" he asked the second boy.

"I am the Duke of York," the boy said.

"Well, I don't believe you, either." Turning to the third scruffy little kid, he asked, "And what's your name?"

At this the lad nudged the other two and said, "Don't worry boys, I won't let you down. Officer, I'm the Archbishop of Canterbury."

The problem with claiming to be the Prince of Wales when you go around knocking off policemen's helmets is that nobody believes you. A noble status demands a disciplined life. Christians find their fulfillment and purpose in being filled with the knowledge of God's will and having an overriding concern to live a life worthy of him.

When we do that, we can't help pleasing him: "And we pray this in order that you may live a life worthy of the Lord and may please him in every way . . ."

I don't know about you, but my greatest ambition in life is to enjoy the smile of his approval. A grin like his can keep me going for eternity!

A Heart in Heaven

*Since, then, you have been raised with Christ, set
your hearts on things above, where Christ is
seated at the right hand of God.*

It's fun watching young men in love. It can be even more fun when the romance is long distance.

You can predict what will happen. There'll be hours of late-night, heart-pounding telephone conversations. The postal service will be overrun with love notes crossing each other in the mail. Pillows will be soaked with tears.

But the most telling symptom is the glazed, faraway look in Romeo's eyes. I'm sure you've seen it. You ask the man a question and you get a blank stare. He's not at home. He's elsewhere, in another land. He's with his sweetheart.

You might say his heart is set on things afar, where Juliet is seated right by the telephone.

Colossians 3:1 has something much grander in view than young love, but perhaps this can get us in the right frame of mind. "Set your hearts on things above, where Christ is seated at the right hand of God," Paul says. That's the thing we have to obey, but before we can understand it, we need to look at the truth that is being stated, then the truth that has been applied.

What is the truth that is being stated? "Christ is seated at the right hand of God," says our verse. That is a fundamental, spiritual, Christian truth.

We all understand that the Bible teaches the Lord Jesus Christ was with the Father before the worlds were made. We know that he assumed our humanity, that he was born a baby in Bethlehem, that he lived for about 33 years, that he died an ignominious death, that on the third day he rose again from the dead, that he ascended to the Father, and that he is seated at the Father's right hand.

Those are basic Christian truths. It is Christian theology. It is either true or untrue, and as we are exposed to these pieces of information, we are required to determine whether they are true or false. If it is true that Christ is seated at the Father's right hand, that means he has an authoritative position. It reminds us that death did not conquer him, but that he conquered death. It reminds us that the risen Lord Jesus is greater than everything that ever defeated a human being, that in him all authority resides and that through him alone can sinful mankind hold audience with God the Father. All that is contained in the statement, "Christ is seated at the right hand of God."

So Christ is seated at the Father's right hand. What has that got to do with us?

Paul says it's important because Christians have been raised with Christ. That's an entirely different matter. It's one thing for me to believe that Jesus Christ, risen from the dead, is seated at the Father's right hand. It's an entirely different thing to see how that has an impact on my own life.

In some way, Paul says I have been raised with Christ. In other words, Christianity is relationship to the living Lord Jesus. My life is inextricably bound up in his life. His life is inextricably bound up in mine. In God's way of looking at things, I am locked into Christ—the same Christ who is in the place of ultimate authority and who has immediate and ready access to the Father. Because I am related to him, I enjoy the identical access!

That will change the way you look at theology! If it is true, then some phenomenal things have taken place. "Wow!" I say, "if Christ is seated at the Father's right hand, and I am locked up in him, then heaven is really my home and earth is only my temporary residence!"

That's the reverse of what we normally think. We tend to think that earth is where the action is and heaven is a dull place 'way out there somewhere, to be dodged as long as possible. We tend to think that life is all about what we can see, touch, taste, and feel. We think it's *earthy*.

But Scripture tells us that if Christ is seated at the Father's right hand and my life is locked up in him, then heaven is my true home and my sojourn here is temporary. That changes my whole orientation to life.

Moreover, if Christ is seated at the Father's right hand, and I have been raised with him, then eternity is the ultimate reality and time is merely transient. That, too, is exactly the opposite of what we tend to think. Our natural tendency is to assume that time is "where it's at." "You only go around once in life, so grab for all the gusto you can," goes the philosophy.

We may not drink their beer, but we listen to their commercials and to a large extent go along with them unthinkingly. We don't stop to realize that they wholly oppose Christian truth, which says it's untrue that we only go around once in life. What really matters is eternity, not time. What you've got here you will leave. Reality is found in eternity and heaven. That's what it means when it says Christ is seated at the Father's right hand and you have been raised with him.

"Do you mean to tell me," you say, "that because I am united with Christ and because he was raised, that my life is bound up in him and in the divine economy I am seated in heaven, that heaven is where I belong, that earth is a temporary residence, that eternity is where it's at, and that time is purely fleeting?"

Yes. Emphatically yes. That's exactly what Paul means.

That being the case, there's a command we need to obey: "Set your hearts on things above." That doesn't make any sense at all until you look at the truth stated, then understand the truth applied. On the other hand, when you understand the truth stated and grasp the truth applied, it's nonsense not to obey.

If it is true that he is raised and I am in him, then my affections need to be locked into Christ, locked into the right hand of the Father, locked into heaven, and locked into eternity. That's where my heart really is. The Lord Jesus said, "Where your treasure is, there will your heart be also."

The converse is also true. Where your heart is, that's where your treasure is going to be.

So ask yourself a question: "Am I clear that Christ is at the Father's right hand? Do I understand that I, united with him, find my life where he is? And do I recognize that when my heart is seated in Christ at the Father's right hand—the place of authority, the place of access to the Father, the place of audience before the Father—that eternity is reality and that heaven is my home?"

When I understand all these things, my heart says, "That's where I find my deepest desires." We see everything in light of this.

Setting our hearts on things above presupposes that we'll guard our affections. How easily our affections can be infected! How often we see young people doing well spiritually until they reach that terribly vulnerable time when their affections start playing tricks on them. Having made a good profession of faith, they fall in love with someone who hasn't the slightest interest in Christ. And what happens? Christ is disregarded. He is disregarded because their affections are unguarded. I have seen it happen far too often.

If we are seated with Christ at the Father's right hand, we also need to guide our affections. We need to guide them so that they are focused on him, so that we understand the truth, so that we tune in to the right wavelength. We need to guide our affections at all times.

Occasionally we need to ask ourselves what grade we would give our affections. What is our heart set on? Are we getting an "A," or are we flunking the course?

Guard your affections. Guide your affections. Grade your affections.

Why should you? Because Christ is seated at the Father's right hand, and you are seated with him. Believe me, there's no better place to be.

The Hidden Source

Set your minds on things above, not on earthly things. For you died, and your life is now hidden with Christ in God.

Few people know that the genius Albert Einstein had more trouble finding his way home from work than he did finding the key to atomic power.

One evening as Einstein sat deep in thought aboard the train that brought him home each night, the porter approached to collect his ticket. Einstein rummaged around in his coat, through his pockets, in his shirt, and everywhere else he could think of. He grew alarmed at his inability to find the ticket.

"That's okay, Dr. Einstein," said the porter, "I know you ride this train every day. I can collect tomorrow."

"That's fine for you, young man," Einstein replied, "but how am I supposed to know where to get off the train without my ticket?"

Paul surely was as single-minded as Einstein, but he dealt with spiritual truth and had a better idea of where he was going. He wanted his readers to join him in the trip. "Set your minds on things above," he writes.

"Hoo boy, these preachers, they do repeat themselves," you say. "He just said to set your hearts on things above, now he says set your minds on things above."

No, Paul is not repeating himself. I admit that preachers do repeat themselves. Sometimes they do it because they haven't prepared—they're winging it. Sometimes they do it because, to their horror, they discover they have more time to fill than they have material to fill it with. At other times they do it by way of emphasis. That's what it is here.

It's one thing to set your heart on things; it's another to set your mind on them. In this passage Paul makes a distinction between your affections and your grasp of truth. "Set your *minds* on things above," he says.

Before we can look into that, we've got to ask ourselves, "What is the truth stated?" It's found in verse 3: "For you died, and your life is now hidden with Christ in God." That's a truth, all right, but it's a little hard to grasp and a little harder to believe. What does he mean?

Let's back up a bit. Earlier in Colossians Paul insisted that not only did Christ die for us, but we died with him. Because it was necessary for Christ to die for some things, it is only appropriate that we should die to those same things.

If I know that I have done many evil and hurtful things in my life; if I am convicted that they are sin and I repent; if I ask forgiveness, understand that Christ died on the cross to forgive me, believe that I have been freely forgiven at the dreadful cost of Christ's life, then how could I merrily go back and engage in the evil that caused Christ's death? If I understand that it was necessary for him to die for these things, then it is only appropriate that I should die to them.

When Paul says "you died," he is really saying that you cannot continue in those evil things because you are so thankful that Christ died to forgive you of them. *You died.*

"Now, just a minute," you say. "All the stuff that I was forgiven, all the the things I used to live for—if I walk away from all that, what would I live for?"

The answer is in the second part of the passage: ". . . for your life is hidden with Christ in God."

There is a secret in your life, a hidden secret. The secret of your life is not all the things you'd rather cover up, not all the things you used to get into, but a wondrously good thing which is hidden. It is hidden in God, and it has to do with Christ.

Have you ever met anybody whose life was hidden with Dow Jones in Wall Street? You say, "I think I did." Have you ever met anybody whose life was hidden with the President in the White House? You say, "Yes, I think I know what you mean." Have you ever come across a kid whose life seems to be hidden with Tina Turner in *MTV*? You say, "Oh-oh, you've been talking to my teen-agers." Do you know anybody whose life was hidden with Jack Daniels in the Main Street Bar? Get the picture?

What is it that makes them tick? Take our man hidden with Dow Jones in Wall Street. Oh, that's not very hidden. It's pretty obvious. He can't wait to grab the paper in the morning, and you know exactly which page he'll turn to first. He'll do this even though he already knows how the Dow Jones did, because he listened to the news the night before. He keeps his radio tuned, too. He can't get past it.

You don't have any problem understanding what keeps some people going—they have a bottle of Jack Daniels within reach wherever they are. You know which filing cabinet they keep it in. Their life is hidden with Jack Daniels.

Or take some teen-agers. Without a constant fix of Tina Turner or the latest from Michael Jackson, they can't keep going. Their life is hidden with *MTV*.

In a similar way, Paul says the lives of Christians are hidden with Christ in God. They're caught up in who he is. They're caught up in what he says. They're caught up with what he has promised. The secret and the source and the content of their life are found in him. It's hidden, but it's where they belong. Christians died a radical termination of the old life. Their life is hidden with Christ in God.

How does that change things?

When your life is hidden with Christ in God, your life's center is Christ. The core of your existence is hidden . . . and you can prove it.

"It used to be that my life was dependent upon my business, then I lost my business. I walked away from it."

"It used to be that my life was dependent upon my family. Then my family let me down."

"It used to be that my life was dependent upon being recognized and upon gaining fame. But lately I've been humbled."

"It used to be that I had all the money I needed, and I could buy whatever I wanted. But I'm afraid I made some bad investments, and it's all gone."

Business gone, family gone, fame and fortune gone. The remarkable thing is that you come across people like this who have gone through similar experiences, and they seem to keep on an even keel. You can chop away at their life—this goes, that goes, and this goes—you keep chopping away, and you wonder, "When on earth will we get them?"

The answer is, you won't. You can't. You can touch all the earthly things, you can touch all the legitimate and all the illegitimate things, but you can never destroy the core at the center of their life. You can't do it for one simple reason: The core in the center of their life is Christ, and he is locked up in God, seated at the Father's right hand, and you can't touch him.

That's why you'll find some people rotting in a cell in the Eastern Bloc, without friends, without family, without church, without Bible, without hymn book, and you can't break their spirit. You can't touch them. Their life is hidden with Christ in God.

Paul tells us to set our minds on things above, not on what we died to. Set your mind on things above, because the core in the center of your life is locked up in Christ, and he is double-wrapped in God. Enemies can get you at any other point, but they can't touch you there.

Think of the worst thing that could happen to you. It's not difficult for any of us. We've all got our pet phobias. What would happen to you if the worst thing that could happen to you happened?

If you're a Christian, you would be rocked, you would be shaken, you would be grief-stricken—but fundamentally, you would be unmoved. Your life is hidden with Christ in God, and you have your mind set on him. You do not need to divert your attention to other things. People who get to that point are remarkable and unusual.

You've heard of people who are so heavenly minded they're no earthly good. Have you met anyone like that? I confess I haven't. Not a one. You see, that's not our problem today.

Our problem is that we are riddled with people who are so earthly minded they're no heavenly use. Paul is not being impractical when he talks about setting your minds on heaven. He's not unrelated to where life is. He knows you've got to live your life down here, and he doesn't promise God will lift you out of the whole thing.

What he insists is that the source and the core in the center of your life is found in Christ, not in earthly things. Therefore, whatever you do, don't allow your attention to be diverted from Christ.

Keep your eyes locked on Christ, obey what he has said, and you'll never have to worry about becoming so earthly minded you're of no heavenly use. You'll be the kind of person who's highly valued both on earth and in heaven.

And we can always use a few more of those.

People in Process

You used to walk in these ways, in the life you once lived. But now you must rid yourselves of all such things as these: anger, rage, malice, slander, and filthy language from your lips. Do not lie to each other, since you have taken off your old self with its practices and have put on the new self, which is being renewed in knowledge in the image of its Creator.

When Jack Eckerd, owner of the Eckerd Drug chain, became a Christian, he knew his life would never be the same. His employees discovered the same thing a short time later.

Chuck Colson relates how Eckerd once walked into one of his stores and spied some soft-core porno magazines for sale. His newly-awakened conscience blared an alert, and he ordered his chief of operations to remove the offensive publications from all his stores.

"But Mr. Eckerd," the man said, "you don't know how much money those magazines bring in! Let me get some information together and show you tomorrow."

Early the next day, the man walked into Eckerd's office and showed him the figures. The magazines *did* earn a substantial profit.

"Take 'em out," Eckerd ordered. "That's an order."

Eckerd understood that when he came to Christ, when he confessed his sins and asked God to forgive him, that a change had to come to his life. He said, in effect, "I am going to take off my old life as if it were an old garment. I'm going to take it off and throw it away. I'm going to put on a new garment, the righteousness of Christ, and I'll stand clothed in him. I have put off the old life, I want to put on the new." That's what Eckerd agreed to when he came to Christ. He saw that it's a major part of what it means to be a Christian.

When you asked to be forgiven of your sins, you put off the old life; it is unthinkable that you should have asked to be forgiven your sins if you fully intended to continue in them. You have taken off the old life like a dirty garment. You have thrown it away, stepped into the shower, and been cleansed by Christ. When you came out, you were dressed splendidly in a new wardrobe.

Don't put your dirty old gear on top of it! Realize that you are being renewed more and more in the image of the Creator.

How were you created in the first place? In the image of God. What happened? The image was marred. What is happening now? You are being renewed, being recreated.

You used to live one way; now you are experiencing an ongoing renewal. If that's true, then it's necessary to clean up your personal life and clean up your social life.

Do you know anyone who is given to fits of rage and anger and malice and slander and abusive language? You say, "Oh, boy, do I!" It's obvious that such a person has all kinds of social problems.

Did you know that one of the best mirrors of your spirituality is your social life? Have you ever thought of that? If your social life is being steered away into the kinds of activities where Christ is not welcome, that tells you something about your heart.

More than that—if your social life is one ongoing fight, rage, anger, malice, and bitterness, just one thing after another, that tells you something about *you*. Not only is your heart wrong, but your mind is set on the wrong thing.

If that's true of you, take action. Clean it up. Get your act together. Why? Because you have taken off the old life and have put on the new. You are being renewed.

You say, "Wow, listening to all of that I feel a bit like a

little old eagle who would like to get his shell back together and hunker down inside it again."

No, you wouldn't. You've tasted of the Lord and seen that he is good. You've tasted enough of him to know you don't want to go back to the old ways.

You say, "Well, maybe I'll just be a little ground eagle then. I'll just flop around down here a bit. I don't want to soar like an eagle."

What a weird eagle you would be!

Don't settle for something as shabby as that. Soar like an eagle! Fly as you were meant to! Whatever it is that is holding you down, put it where it belongs and begin to live in Christ.

Once the wind is whistling through your sleek wings and you survey the majestic vista below, you'll be glad you did. I guarantee it.

Realize, though, that these changes won't come into your life overnight. Sometimes it takes awhile.

One day about 100 years ago, Phillips Brooks, a pastor reknowned as a powerful speaker and as the author of the Christmas carol, "O Little Town of Bethlehem," was pacing fretfully in his office and muttering to himself. A friend walked into his study, saw his preoccupation, and asked what troubled him.

"The trouble is that I'm in a hurry, and God isn't," Brooks replied.

That's often our trouble, too. We want immediate action when God seems content to move slowly. Sometimes agonizingly so.

Have you ever noticed something like this? You think Mrs. Brown should have mastered by now a problem that's plagued her for years. Mrs. Brown thinks Mr. Smith should be ashamed of making so little progress in some other area. And Mr. Smith thinks that any *real* Christian ought to be able to tame a quick temper (like the one you've got).

People want change to come quickly . . . especially when it's change in someone else. But notice that Paul says believers are a people *in process*. Believers have put on the new self "which is *being renewed* in knowledge in the image of its Creator." Notice the tense! While there is a very real sense in which Christians have been redeemed as an accomplished fact, there is another sense in which being renewed is a process. In terms of forgiveness your salvation is finished, complete, but in terms of being changed your salvation is an ongoing procedure.

This is something that both Christians and critics of Christians sometimes misunderstand or ignore. Paul says Christians are people who *are being renewed* in the image of the Creator. It's a process requiring time, which will only be complete when believers stand before Christ. Scripture says when we stand before him we will see him and will be like him.

We need to understand this about ourselves and about each other. Do you know why? When we understand we're imperfect and incomplete and that we don't have it all together, it's amazing how tolerant we can become of each other. If we expect everybody to be perfect, to have it all together, and if we suggest we've already arrived, then there's no room for making mistakes and every excuse for being hard and harsh and unrelenting and unforgiving.

On the other hand, if we know that we are people in process, then forgiveness is in order, tolerance is in order, openness is in order. If it were not for this, it would be nonsense for Paul in verse 12 to talk about compassion, kindness, humility, gentleness, patience, forbearing one another, and forgiving one another.

Because we are people in process, we can respond to each other in gentleness and compassion. Because we are redeemed, the Lord is in the process of renewing us. That should be respected. We should respect the struggle we're all going through. We should respect the aspirations we have but don't always achieve. We should remember that God is still working on us.

Some of us like bumper stickers. I know, because I see them all the time (and some of them I wish I didn't). It seems to me that one of the most appropriate is surely, "Please be patient, God isn't finished with me yet." That's the theme.

When you come across a group of believers that understands they are a people in process, you will find a congregation with a warm, generous spirit. If, on the other hand, you should uncover a group that doesn't appreciate the process, you're sure to find a spirit so hard and harsh as to shatter concrete. Or people.

If you are a believer, you are a person in process. As is the person on your right. And on your left. And in front of you or behind you. Do yourself a favor and treat them as the incomplete, maturing saints they are. Remember, God isn't finished with them yet.

Or with you!

Working Out

1. The phrase in Colossians 3:1 translated "set your hearts on things above" comes from a Greek word which literally means "seek," "try to obtain," "desire to possess." The same word is used in Matthew 6:33, where Jesus speaks of God's kingdom and tells us to "*seek* first his kingdom and his righteousness, and all these things will be given to you as well." Paul uses the word in Romans 2:6-8 when he writes, "God 'will give to each person according to what he has done.' To those who by persistence in doing good *seek* glory, honor and immortality, he will give eternal life. But for those who are self-seeking and who reject the truth and follow evil, there will be wrath and anger."

A. What things are promised in each of these passages?

B. In the verses surrounding each of these passages, a warning is given. What are these warnings?

C. If you wanted to discover what things a person was "seeking after," how would you go about it? Would you find out where they spent their time? Would you try to get a peek at their checkbook? Would you ask their friends what seemed to get them most excited? Would you listen to see what they most often talked about? How would you determine what they were seeking in life? Make a list of the questions you would ask.

When you have your list prepared, apply it to your own life. What things are you "seeking after," according to your own investigation?

2. Listed below are six things that Colossians 3:8-9 says believers must avoid. Look up each word's definition in a dictionary, and on the blank lines which follow each item, write down the definitions you find. Do you need to work harder at getting rid of any of them?

A. Anger _____

B. Rage _____

C. Malice _____

D. Slander _____

E. Obscenities _____

F. Lying _____

Second Wind

1. Matthew 5:43-48
   To whom does Jesus say we should give our love? What does he think of those who don't?

2. Galatians 5:13-15
   How does Paul say we best demonstrate our freedom in Christ?

3. 2 Timothy 3:1-5
   Will it be easy to live a life pleasing to God the nearer we get to Christ's Second Coming?

4. James 3:13-18
   What effect do the "wise" people described in this passage have on those around them?

5. 2 Peter 1:5-9
   What keeps Christians from becoming ineffective in their faith? How do you acquire it?

III
Christian Relationships

Adopting a Team Strategy

Who Can I Count On?

[Christ] is the head of the body, the church ...
Colossians 1:18

Do not ... [lose] connection with the Head,
from whom the whole body,
supported and held together by its ligaments and sinews,
grows as God causes it to grow.
Colossians 2:18, 19

My purpose is that they may be ... united in love,
so that they may have the full riches
of complete understanding.
Colossians 2:2

Here there is no Greek or Jew,
circumcised or uncircumcised,
barbarian, Scythian, slave or free,
but Christ is all, and is in all.
Therefore, as God's chosen people, holy and dearly loved,
clothe yourselves with compassion, kindness, humility,
gentleness and patience.
Bear with each other and forgive whatever grievances
you may have against one another.
Forgive as the Lord forgave you.
And over all these virtues put on love,
which binds them all together in perfect unity.
Let the peace of Christ rule in your hearts,
since as members of one body you were called to peace.
And be thankful.
Let the word of Christ dwell in you richly
as you teach and admonish one another with all wisdom,
and as you sing psalms, hymns and spiritual songs
with gratitude in your hearts to God.
And whatever you do, whether in word or deed,
do it all in the name of the Lord Jesus,
giving thanks to God the Father through him.
Colossians 3:11-17

Growing Together

I f you want to become a better basketball player, what do you do? You find a team and play on it.

If you want to learn Scandinavian cooking, what do you do? You find some old pros and imitate their technique.

If you want to grow as a parent, or as a teacher, or as a pianist, or as a manicurist, what do you do? You find people who have the same interest and long experience and you spend time with them. That's how we grow in almost any field you can name.

So why is it that when it comes to spiritual growth, we abandon the process? Why is it that so many folks consider the church irrelevant to their spiritual growth and never see it as the fundamental, basic aspect of the process that it truly is? Their quest for spiritual maturity is stymied, but they never know why. It's really not such a mystery.

The fact is, if you want to grow, you must be involved in the church.

Now, there are many pictures of the church in Scripture, but one of the best known and loved is of the church as a body with Christ as its head. We are part of a fellowship where Christ is connecting all the members together. He is coordinating by the sinews and the ligaments the supply of life that comes from his headship, deeply involving us in the life of a believing fellowship under his control, connecting us to others, coordinating us in our lives.

We dare not turn our eyes off Christ, but neither must we lose sight of the task to which Christ committed himself—the building of his church. When we remember this, we will treat with tremendous respect the whole idea of being part of a body of believers who acknowledge Christ as their head and who regard themselves as being part of his body.

Christianity is not lived in isolation, "just me and the Lord." Christianity is lived within a community of believers. Every community must have a coordinated membership. Chaos results when everybody does his own thing.

Integrated, coordinated living in the fellowship of believers presumes that the people who would submit to the Lord also are prepared to submit to each other. It's at this very point that a lot of people in the church get into trouble.

When they find that things aren't going their way, they pick up their ball and head for another church. Instead of resolving the problem by displaying a submissive attitude, they simply take their rebellious disposition to another church. It's only a matter of time until the same dreary cycle repeats itself.

I never try to persuade people to stay at Elmbrook if they want to leave, any more than I try to persuade people to come who don't want to. My philosophy is very simple. There are two doors on this church. The front door says, "Whosoever will, may come," and the back door says, "Whosoever won't, may go." We must feel very, very free in between.

What really goes on in the pews when God's people gather together? How do people who sit in the pew behave in light of the fact that they are related to the Lord Jesus Christ, the head of the church? Just what should be our view of the pew?

Let's take a look at what Paul has to say about living and working in the church of Christ Jesus.

The Lone Ranger Should Join a Church

*My purpose is that they may be . . . united in love,
so that they may have the full riches of complete
understanding.*

An American was telling a group of friends about a trip he'd recently taken to Africa. He'd gone there with a Christian relief organization to find and tap fresh water supplies for poor villages.

One day he and his African friends were traveling by jeep from one village to another. They had journeyed a fair distance when they had to stop because a small bridge on their route had collapsed.

The American took one look at the problem and thought to himself, *No big deal. It should only take a couple of minutes to repair, and we can be on our way.*

Two Africans got out of the jeep and inspected the broken bridge. Patiently they began discussing a possible remedy. This went on for ten minutes, then fifteen, then twenty, then half an hour. It was obvious the two did not agree on the best solution to the problem, and equally clear they were prepared to quietly talk through the dilemma. The American, glancing at his watch, grew impatient.

For Pete's sake, guys, one of you just take charge and tell the other what to do, he thought. *We don't have time for all this!*

But the Africans continued their conversation, and only after coming to some sort of agreement did they get the bridge repaired. Once they went to work, the repairs took but a few minutes.

The American was steaming. He was about to lay into one of his African hosts when the man explained what had just taken place. Neither African had wanted to offend the other by insisting on his method of bridge first aid. Either method would have worked, and both would have taken about the same amount of time, but these men treasured friendship above time management. In their culture, maintaining good relationships was more important than maintaining timely schedules.

The American gulped.

Here I came to teach, he thought, *and I'm the one who's learning.*

Those African men knew that one of the best ways to encourage a brother is to be united in spirit with him. That's exactly what the apostle Paul taught the Colossian church, and it's a lesson we desperately need to learn. Paul wanted the church to be united in love.

There is a very real sense in which we cannot grow spiritually in isolation. Paul says, "I want individuals lovingly united with others in order that they might have complete understanding." How does this work?

You can grow to a certain extent on your own. You can study on your own. You can have devotions on your own. You can do a lot of things on your own—and you should—but there are many, many things you need to do corporately if you are to "have the full riches of understanding."

Look at it this way. If you operate all on your own with the Lord Jesus, then you are to a very large extent limited to your own capacity. If, on the other hand, you relate to the Lord Jesus in the fellowship of others, the discoveries they have made can benefit you and your discoveries can enrich them. You'll begin to knock the rough edges off each other and encourage each other to work things through.

One of my favorite times of the week is Monday morning. That's right, Monday morning. I know that most pastors take Mondays off, but we don't at Elmbrook. We gather early on Monday morning as a staff to study the Scripture and discuss theology.

You know why it's one of my favorite times? It's because I know that the more I know, the more I know that I don't know. I'm so grateful for the gifted, godly men and women that God has gathered around me. He has allowed my life to become part of theirs, and theirs to become part of mine.

We knock the corners off each other. We knock the rough edges off each other. We make great theological pronouncements, and the others fall off their chairs laughing at the very idea that we can be so stupid. What an encouragement this can be.

We are united in love in order that we might come to a full understanding.

How does this work for you? Some Christians think they can get along just fine by having their morning devotions for a few minutes and coming to church once on a Sunday morning, and that's it. It's all very isolated.

They're wrong.

Continue to do those things, by all means! But understand that you need a spiritual environment in which you relate to others. When you are united in love with others in the church, *then* you can begin to learn the full riches of understanding.

There's an expression afoot today that's become quite popular. It's called "one-on-one discipleship." Goodness only knows where it came from, but it certainly didn't come from the Bible. It's not a biblical concept. One-on-one is basketball, not discipleship.

You don't disciple people one-on-one. You clone people one-on-one. I get letters from people all the time asking, "Can I come and spend six months in your church, and would you disciple me?"

I always write back and say, "No."

"Why not?" they ask.

"Because I don't want any more like me," I reply. "I don't want any Stuart Briscoe clones. What I'd like is to have you come in and be part of the team, be part of the fellowship. You'll pick up something from him and something from her, and you'll see how what she is better reflects who Christ is than what I am does."

As we discover what it is to be united in love with members of the body of Christ, we begin to grow in our understanding of the mystery of Christ.

Let's face it, people who are serious about their spiritual lives will freely admit that the deeper they get, the more shallow they discover their experience to be. Whenever you come across a believer who is satisfied, you know you've come across a shallow one.

There is so much of God to know. There is so much in me to be changed. There is so much in the world to do. If I'm satisfied with knowing God minimally—with allowing minimal change in my life and making minimal impact on my world—then I am a living testimonial to my own shallowness.

But if I begin to think in terms of being united in love with others so that I might come to a fuller understanding of things, then I will make it a priority to be involved in the church. Why? Because I know how far I have to go.

Do you want to grow spiritually? Do you want to become more and more like Christ? Do you want the strength of character and depth of understanding and gladness of spirit that only come with a maturing faith?

Then make sure you're in a church environment where you are growing in unity with others so that everyone may attain to the full riches of complete understanding.

I guarantee you that God isn't looking for any Lone Ranger Christians. The ones who try it look more like Lonely Ranger Christians to me. You don't need that, and neither do I.

So let's get involved! I need you, and you need me. That's what the church is all about.

Barriers Are for Bridging

Here there is no Greek or Jew, circumcised or
uncircumcised, barbarian, Scythian, slave or
free, but Christ is all, and is in all.

One of the most awesome major league baseball teams in history was the Oakland Athletics of the early 1970s. The team won three straight world championships, something no one else has done since.

You never would have guessed it had you visited their locker room.

They fought like cats and dogs. They needled each other. They fumed at each other. They scuffled with each other. They called each other names. They played nasty tricks on each other.

But when they got out on the playing field, they were nearly unbeatable. Why?

Because when it came time for the game to begin, they put everything else aside and focused on baseball.

Paul had something very like that in mind in Colossians 3:11. He says the people of the pew are focused on Christ: "Here there is no Greek or Jew, circumcised or uncircumcised, barbarian, Scythian, slave or free, but *Christ is all, and in all.*"

What characterizes the community of believers? They are focused on Christ. "Christ is all that matters," is one way to paraphrase it.

Think about that. Believers come together because of who they are, because of what has happened in their lives, because of where they have come from, because of their circumstances. They have all kinds of varying interests and ideas. But when they come together as believers, they must take all those ideas and subject them to the one predominant idea, which is "Christ is all that matters." He is the focus of our attention; he is the One whom we seek to honor and to love and to serve.

So Christ is all. But he's also *in* all.

Believers know that a truly reborn and redeemed person is indwelt by the living Christ through the Holy Spirit. Whatever may be happening in their lives, they must see that the Lord Jesus Christ is alive in them. He is also alive in others. It is the same Lord living and working in every believer. That is what bonds them together.

It is true that diverse interests, prejudices, and priorities in any group are bound to generate problems. If, however, these things become secondary, not primary—first, because Christ is all that matters, and second, because members of the body see Christ in all his people and recognize that sooner or later he will bring things together—then Paul says the fellowship of believers will flourish.

The apostle wasn't just talking theory here. He had to overcome all kinds of barriers in the church at Colossae. I see at least four.

Racial and ethnic differences. The Jews and Greeks had profoundly different roots and were proud of their racial and ethnic histories. The Jews, especially, had a profound sense of history. You can't read Jewish literature without hearing about the Exodus. You can't read Jewish literature without running into Moses and the Ten Commandments. The Jews go back—way, way, way back. They are people of a deep, rich, proud heritage.

The Greeks had developed a superb culture and heritage of their own. If you want a feel for how superb it was, visit Athens. Read their literature and their tragedies, see their architecture and their culture, hear what their philosophers had to say. You'll declare, "What a profound people they were."

But Jews and Greeks were at loggerheads . . . until Christ touched both Jew and Greek and brought them together. In the fellowship at Colossae, who was a Jew and who was a Greek? Who cared? Christ was the focus.

Religious differences. Some members of the church believed that to be truly born of the Spirit, you had to adhere to all the niceties of Judaism, including circumcision. Others said that wasn't necessary; in Christ, circumcision availed absolutely nothing. "So don't do it," they insisted.

Paul had to get both groups to see the uselessness of focusing on the outward rites of religion. Neither circumcision nor uncircumcision mattered. What mattered was Christ.

Cultural differences. The Greeks were an arrogant bunch. Now, some people are arrogant and you can't figure out why. Others are arrogant and you say, "I understand." The Greeks are in the latter category. The Romans thought so, too, for they more or less adopted Greek culture and spread it over the world. The Greeks and Romans were buddies. They lumped the rest of the world into one category—barbarian.

There was one particular group of barbarians called Scythians. They were the most uncultured, uncouth bunch of woodies you'd ever meet. Somehow or another these unlettered, uncultured, uncouth woodies from Scythia had come to Colossae, and would you believe—horror of horrors—they got converted, to the intense distaste and concern of all the cultured and lettered Greeks.

But the apostle Paul, who is as cultured and as lettered as any of them, says, "So what? Does it really matter if they are uncouth? Does it matter if they are uncultured or unlettered? Who's worried about those things? They're all secondary; what really matters is focusing on Christ."

Social differences. Both slaves and free men attended church in Colossae. It's hard to imagine a more profound social distinction than that. Yet they worshiped together. We learn more about this dimension of the Colossian church through the little letter of Philemon, which Paul wrote at the same time he penned his letter to Colossae. If you really want to study your Bible, begin with Philemon—it's the shortest book in the New Testament, next to 2 and 3 John. You'll love it. It's a very personal letter.

Philemon was a businessman in the church at Colossae. As was normal in those days, he had slaves. One of them,

Onesimus, ran off to Rome, knowing that the penalty for escape was death. One day this runaway slave bumped into Paul. Before long he was converted.

"What should I do now?" he asked the apostle.

"You must go back home and face the music," Paul told him.

"Oh, no, I'm not going back there," Onesimus said.

"Yes, you are," replied the apostle. "You're a Christian; go and face the music. I'll write a letter for you."

So Paul wrote a letter, gave it to Onesimus, and packed him off to Philemon. That letter is one of the warmest, most gracious notes you'll ever read. And what Paul says in that letter is this: "Forgive Onesimus and receive him. He was a runaway slave, but now he is a brother beloved. He was not good at all to you, but now he is highly profitable to me."

If you had visited that church weeks later, you would have seen Philemon and Onesimus sitting together in the church of Colossae. How on earth could those two get along? Oh, they did a lot more than get along—they warmly embraced each other. How? They focused on Christ.

Occasionally I hear rumbles in my own church over social distinctions. Some groups make sure they never get together with other groups. It's hard for me to understand. I'd love to take these people by the hand and drop them in the church at Colossae, where they'd find both slaves and slave owners. Paul says when you focus on Christ, social distinctions don't count for much. Amazing.

If there is one thing in the church of Jesus Christ that I long for, quite frankly it is for people in the pews to understand that when they focus on Christ, all barriers are transcended. Lose your focus on Christ, and there will be as many barriers as people. Someone has said, "get a group of twelve Christians together and you'll have thirteen opinions." That's true. But if those people can focus on Christ and begin to regard all other things as secondary, then they can be knit together as a community of believers.

What is it that splits a church? It is people who major on racial barriers, religious differences, cultural niceties, or social prejudices. Some believers confuse a meeting of minds with a butting of heads. We have to recognize that when our focus is on Christ—when he is allowed to work in each of our lives—then these real barriers can be transcended in him.

I once met a professional bull rider in the rodeo. "You don't mind if I eat with my hat on, do you?" he asked. For a professional bull rider, I don't mind anything. He can sit on the table if he likes.

"So, what do you do?" he asked.

"I do some preaching and that kind of thing," I replied.

"Oh, you're a pastor, are you?"

"Yes, I am."

"Do you have hymn books in your church?"

"Yes, we have hymn books in our church."

"I wouldn't join that church."

"Really? Why not?"

"You can't worship God with hymn books."

"Why not?"

"How could you raise your hands and still hold a hymn book?"

"Well, you could raise the hymn book up in the air with one hand and stick the other one up if you wanted to."

"No, I wouldn't worship there."

Do you see his problem? His problem was style of worship. Frankly, I don't care if people raise their hands or don't raise their hands. What does it matter? If that is an expression of worship for some, great! If it isn't for others, great! When Christ is all and in all, using hymnals or raising hands is secondary.

Let's pause a moment to look at *our* fellowship. Are we a fellowship of believers that can honestly say our focus is on Christ? Yes, we look at things differently, we think about things differently, we feel differently about all kinds of things—but do we allow these differences to take our attention off *him*?

Who Can I Count On?

Get your eyes off Christ, and you'll be in all kinds of trouble. Keep your eyes on him, and you can survive almost anything in the fellowship of believers.

Even hymn books.

Mopheads and Toothbrushes Welcome

*Therefore, as God's chosen people, holy and
dearly loved, clothe yourselves with compassion,
kindness, humility, gentleness and patience.
Bear with each other and forgive whatever
grievances you may have against one another.
Forgive as the Lord forgave you. And over all these
virtues put on love, which binds them all together
in perfect unity.*

We are all accustomed to speaking of the Jews as God's chosen people. It's scriptural. The Bible insists that the Jews were indeed the chosen people.

When you take that into account, there's something especially fascinating about what Paul says concerning the church in Colossians 3:12-14. It's hidden just under the surface: ". . . God's chosen people, holy and dearly loved." All those expressions are picked straight out of Deuteronomy 7:6-8, where they apply to Israel.

The New Testament calls the church "the Israel of God" (Galatians 6:16). Many of the things that applied to Israel as a chosen people—holy and specially loved by God—now apply to the church. Why? Because in the same way that God wanted a people, a community, which was readily identified with him in Old Testament days, so he wants a people, a community, which is readily identifiable with him now. That new community is the church.

The people of the pew are a unique community.

Christians must understand that they are called not only to relate to Christ, but to a community of believers. God doesn't

167

just want individuals running around the place, he wants a clearly distinguishable, distinctive people—dearly loved, set apart, chosen to be his people. That is why an individual Christian should always be identified with a specific community of believers. We are not only to model our Christianity individually, we are to model it corporately as a people of God.

This unique people of God is to demonstrate unique behavior. Community behavior in the church is not like community behavior outside the church. Community behavior in the church is characterized by Christian graces. Paul says believers are to be "clothed" with them, which suggests the need to put out some effort. Notice the sorts of things that Christians are to be clothed with: ". . . compassion, kindness, humility, gentleness and patience." These are nearly the same things listed in the "Fruit of the Spirit" passage in Galatians 5. Christian graces blossom in our lives as the Holy Spirit works in and through us and as we make an effort to cooperate with him.

Let's ask ourselves a question. Am I characterized by compassion and kindness and humility and gentleness and patience? By nature no, I'm not. I know I'm not. Enough people have told me so. And yet it would be true to say that the Spirit of God is working on the old man.

Would it be true to say that just once in awhile you get a glimmer of progress in this area? I profoundly hope so. I hope all of us can be honest and say, "Yes, I am lacking in compassion. I'm not very kind. I'm not very humble, either. I thought I was. I got all humble and then I got proud of it."

Maybe we can look at ourselves and say, "This is what I am, but by the grace of God changes are taking place. I'm working on it. I'm troubled and concerned about it. I want to be part of a community characterized by these things. I know it's going to take the work of the Spirit in my life and my cooperative effort with him."

Yet days will come when something happens in the church that provokes you. Isn't it easy to get fed up with God's people? The problem, quite frankly, is that the church of Jesus Christ is made up exclusively of redeemed sinners. And these wretched sinners—I'm one of them—have an awful habit of showing their true colors. If we're going to come down like a ton of bricks on everybody who shows his true colors, then there is going to be an awful pile of bricks around the place. It's amazing how far a little forbearance will go.

I'm not saying we turn a blind eye to things. I'm not saying we shrug our shoulders or let anything go. Christian grace isn't license. It's an attitude that begins to bind together the most disparate groups of people—Jews, Greeks, slaves, freemen, circumcised, uncircumcised, Scythian, barbarian, educated, cultured—the whole bunch together.

How on earth are you going to get people this dissimilar into one new community? You won't, unless there is Christian grace and Christian attitude . . . *and* Christian action.

Notice what Paul says: "Forgive whatever grievances you may have against one another. Forgive as the Lord forgave you."

Anybody who's been around the church for a while can talk about forgiveness. We've all heard so much about it. It's easy to shrug it aside. Recently I heard a new wrinkle on the idea that renewed my appreciation for what it involves.

It came from a TV program about stock car drivers. You say, "That will be real helpful on forgiveness, I'm sure." Well, it was. As a group sat in class learning how to be stock car drivers, the lecturer said that the first thing to remember about stock car racing was this: Concrete walls are very unforgiving.

I pricked up my ears. "Concrete walls are very unforgiving."

Let's turn it around. Unforgiving people remind you of concrete walls. You've got a bit of momentum in your life, you've gone off track a little, you're heading for trouble—but fortunately, somebody has put a concrete wall in your way. KABOOM! And that solves everything.

No, it doesn't. It just makes things ten times worse.

One day I would like to go up in a fighter plane and land on the deck of an aircraft carrier in a rough sea. Now, I've gotten close. I've landed in a helicopter on a giant, ocean-going tanker off Capetown. That was fun, but a bit tame.

Just imagine coming in on one of those fighters. You see the aircraft carrier down below, its flight deck the size of a postage stamp. "I sure hope they know what they're doing," you say. You swoop down at two hundred miles per hour, and as you hit the flight deck, you discover, fortunately, that someone's built a concrete wall across your path. KABOOM! As you splatter yourself on the windshield, you moan, "Well, at least I'm not in the ocean."

No, they don't build concrete walls across flight decks. Do you know what they do? They string a cable across the deck, designed to catch a hook on the underside of the plane. The cable has all kinds of give in it and takes the heat out of the plane's speed. It takes the steam out of it and brings the thing to a halt.

I want to suggest that the difference between forgiving and unforgiving is the difference between concrete walls and flexible cable. Forgiving is something that needs to go on in the fellowship of believers all the time, because there is always somebody upset with somebody. There's always some evangelical nose out of joint somewhere. And the last thing that bent evangelical noses need is to be rubbed into concrete walls.

So far so good. But what binds all these things together? What keeps them functioning as they ought? "Over all these virtues," writes Paul, "put on love, which binds them all together in perfect unity." Oh, I love that word "unity"! But don't confuse it with "unison." If the church of Jesus Christ thinks unity means that everybody must look the same, think the same, and act the same, they are going to produce the most boring bunch of peas in a pod you'll ever see.

Years ago I was saying something like this at a conference. I was describing how delightful it was to have some of the wild and woolly kinds from the counter-culture as part of our fellowship. One of the pastors sitting in the audience couldn't tolerate it any longer. Suddenly he shouted out, "Can you tell me why all these young people want to grow their hair so they look like mopheads?" He just shouted out in the middle of my talk. I said, "No, sir, I can't."

But as I looked at them and saw a row of overweight pastors, all with charcoal gray suits, light gray ties, white shirts, and crew cuts, I continued. "No, sir, I can't tell you why these kids want to grow their hair so they look like mopheads. But it's the same reason you fellows all want to look like big, black, fat toothbrushes."

They never asked me back.

You know, I like mopheads sitting next to toothbrushes. I really do. It gives us a chance to learn how to forgive, to forbear.

Here's the rule: When in doubt about forgiving, it's a case of one-give, two-give, three-give, four-give. You got it. A little, subtle pun to end the chapter.

Things to Do

Let the peace of Christ rule in your hearts, since
as members of one body you were called to peace.
And be thankful. Let the word of Christ dwell in
you richly as you teach and admonish one
another with all wisdom, and as you sing psalms,
hymns and spiritual songs with gratitude in your
hearts to God.

I wish I never heard conversations like the following, but I'm afraid they occur all the time:

"I'm going to do such and such a thing, even though some people tell me it's wrong."

"How can you do that?"

"I've got peace about it."

"Doesn't the fact that God tells you not to do it mean anything?"

"I've got peace about it."

"But Scripture says it's wrong!"

"I don't care. I've got peace about it."

These confused people nullify an objective truth by their subjective experience of peace. Now, it's true that Paul says we are to be governed by peace: "Let the peace of Christ rule in your hearts." He did not, however, mean "peace" as an individual, personal, subjective thing.

The problem is that subjective "peace" can be nothing more than the chloroforming of the conscience. Give your conscience a hard time long enough, say no to your conscience long enough, tell it "phooey" long enough, and in the end your conscience will tell you to go ahead and live as you please. You can call that "peace" if you want to, but that's not what Paul's writing about here.

When Paul mentions "peace," he is talking about a sense of order in relationships between Christians. Believers are called to orderly behavior. We are not called to hassling, we are not called to having fights. We are not called to arguments or cliques or schisms or feuds. We are called to none of that. We in the church must allow our lives to be governed by peace.

This peace, Paul says, is to have a traveling buddy named "thankfulness." One evening at Elmbrook we held a quarterly meeting of pastors, elders, and deacons. We had a great meeting. The last hour was devoted to people's standing up and declaring one thing for which they were thankful, sharing one new thing they had seen God do in our fellowship during the previous year. We had to cut it off after an hour. One person after another kept jumping up and saying "this is new," "this is what God is doing," "this is what I am thankful for." You walk out on air after a meeting like that.

It's amazing what a dash of thankfulness will do. It's amazing what a commitment to peace and order in the fellowship will do. It begins to produce the body of Christ.

None of it "just happens." It only happens in a fellowship of believers permeated by the Word. "Let the word of Christ dwell in you richly as you teach and admonish one another with all wisdom," Paul writes.

That means that when you pick a church to join (horrible thought that we do it that way, but let's accept it), make absolutely certain you know its priorities. Is it a community of believers that holds high the Word of Christ? Is it committed to allowing that Word to dwell richly within it and among it? Find a church that deviates from the Word, and you've found a church on the way out.

Praise is another element which ought constantly to enrich the community of believers: "Let the word of Christ dwell in you richly as you teach and admonish one another with all wisdom, and as you sing psalms, and hymns and spiritual songs with gratitude in your hearts to God."

The fellowship of believers is a praising community where people who can sing beautifully, sing beautifully; and those who just sing, just sing; and those who have voices like crows with laryngitis croak to the glory of God. But nobody just sits there like an old sourpuss, looking as if they had lost their last friend, having had their breakfast of onions.

Some have tried to differentiate between "psalms" and "hymns" and "spiritual songs," but I think such distinctions are more a work of creativity than of fact. We know that the Lord Jesus and his disciples, after the first communion, sang a hymn and went out to the Mount of Olives. And we know exactly what they would sing at that particular time—it would be Psalms 115, 116, 117, and 118. The "hymns" they sang were psalms.

We also know what songs will be sung in heaven, because Revelation tells us. "They sang a new song," it says, and even gives the lyrics. At other times when we read the word "hymn" in our English Bibles, it's actually from the Greek word "psalm." I mention all this just to say we shouldn't be too picky about making exact distinctions.

Still, Paul gives us one interesting insight into this issue from 1 Corinthians 14. In that letter he told the Corinthians that when they came together, some would have a word and some would have a hymn and some would have a prophecy and some would have a tongue. Small groups of Corinthians got together, and in the free-flowing worship time that ensued, someone might step forward and announce, "I wrote a hymn. I'd like to sing it." And the people would say, "Did you bring your guitar?" And he would reply, "No, but I've got my lute." And so they would all get out their lutes (whatever you do with a lute, I don't know) and would sing the hymn.

It would take a long time for churches like Elmbrook, with its 5,000 attenders, to invite everyone to come up to the platform one after another and sing the hymns they'd written that week. That's the idea in this passage, though. It's an invitation for everyone to get involved.

"Oh, I couldn't write a hymn!"

You couldn't? Have you ever tried?

"Oh, I couldn't write a song!"

You couldn't? Have you ever tried?

"I could never sing!"

You couldn't? Have you ever tried?

Listen, the community of believers is a praising community. It is a group of people rooted in the psalms and rooted in the Scriptures who love to join together to sing God's praises with a heart of gratitude. Enrichment is the natural result.

But Paul isn't finished yet. There's one last thing the people of the pew need in order to fully discover their heritage: They are committed to glorifying God. "Whatever you do," Paul says in a great catch-all verse, "whether in word or deed, do it all in the name of the Lord Jesus, giving thanks to God the Father through him."

That means that what we do and what we say must be intended to represent Christ appropriately. Have you got that? When we do things or say things in the fellowship of believers, let's ask ourselves, "Does this adequately represent Christ?" If it doesn't, don't say it. If it doesn't represent love for Christ, don't do it.

A good question to ask is this: Will doing or saying this thing be a real privilege for which I can thank God? If you're about to say something—knowing full well you can't thank God for the privilege of saying it—don't say it. If you plan to do something but know deep down in your heart you can't thank God for the privilege of doing it, don't do it.

Let's put this positively. Whatever you do in word or deed, do it all in the name of the Lord Jesus, giving thanks to God the Father through him.

When this happens, what is said and taught and done in the community of believers begins to glorify God and honor Christ. Only then do we begin to understand—and enjoy!—life in the pew.

Working Out

Colossians 3:9-17

1. Divide a clean sheet of paper into two columns. At the top of one column, write "Things to avoid." At the top of the other column, write "Things to do." Now read through Colossians 3:9-17, looking for commands in each of those two categories. To the right of each item you find, place a small box. After you have completed your lists, go through each column and place a check by every item you think you need to work on. For example:

Things to Avoid   **Things to Do**
Lying (v. 9) _____   *Be kind (v. 12)* _____
Favoritism (v. 11) __X__   *Be humble (v. 12)* __X__

When you have completed your list and have "graded" yourself, make room at the bottom of the page for a few personal statements explaining specifically what you are going to do to improve in these weak areas you've just identified. For example:

I will try to break out of my "clique" by inviting a new couple in the church over for dinner next Sunday.

Every time in the next month that I find myself boasting about one of my accomplishments, I will put $5 in a special fund to be given away to a local charity.

2. Very often in some Christian circles you will hear slogans such as "Let go and let God," which remind us that enjoying a successful Christian life depends upon tapping God's strength and not relying upon our own. But these slogans also may lull us into thinking that we needn't put out any effort at all—we may think that God will simply bypass our wills and energy.

Look again at Colossians 3:5, 8, 12, 14, 15, 16. Notice how often Paul uses words that demand personal action and effort in cooperation with God's power. List all of Paul's commands in these verses that show how the apostle directed his Colossian friends to put out some effort in living the Christian life.

3. The church is taking some hard knocks lately. Take five minutes to write down several things you're thankful for in your own church. Then let someone else know about them.

Second Wind

1. Acts 2:42-47
   Why did the early church grow so rapidly? Can we imitate any of its practices?

2. 1 Corinthians 12:12-31
   Get the "feel" of this passage by imagining that for one day each part of your own body could talk. What would each part say to the others? Apply that to your church.

3. Ephesians 2:11-22
   What did Christ destroy, and what did he build? What do we destroy, and what do we build?

4. Hebrews 10:24-25
   Name one major reason we should meet together to encourage each other.

5. 1 Peter 2:4-12
   Name one purpose for the church as Peter presents it.

How Does My Family Fit In?

Wives, submit to your husbands, as is fitting in the Lord.
Husbands, love your wives and do not be harsh with them.
Children, obey your parents in everything,
for this pleases the Lord.
Fathers, do not embitter your children,
or they will become discouraged.
Colossians 3:18-21

Family Living

I t is a well-known fact that families today are in deep, dire trouble. Even Christian families. When relationships sour and marriages get shaky, all too often Christian people do exactly what we expect of unbelievers. They split. They say, "Let's call it quits." They get divorces, divide up everything, divvy up the care of the children, and head in different directions.

This is deeply troubling, because clearly it is not an adequate response to a dreadful problem. It's my contention that underlying many family and marital problems are basic spiritual problems. Let me put it another way.

If you as a believer are having tensions in your marriage, if you as a believer are having problems in your family, don't look first of all for secular advice. Don't look first of all for secular solutions. Assume there's a good chance that underlying your marital or family problems are some major spiritual problems, and that if those spiritual difficulties can be ironed out, your family problems may well take care of themselves.

Do not misunderstand; this is no rap against marriage and family counseling. Neither is it a rap against Christian family psychological counseling. I totally support what professionals in those fields are doing. They're vital to helping solve many of the problems we confront.

My contention is simply this: I am convinced that many, many marriage and family problems are really problems of disobedience. The only solution to many of these problems is down-to-earth, gutsy obedience, lived out in the power of the Holy Spirit. Or to put it in simple terms: There are spiritual answers to many of the marriage and family problems confronting us.

If that were not true, why would the apostle Paul put this practical teaching on family living in the context of a spiritual and theological treatise? For that is exactly what he does. The apostle sets his practical teaching on family life in the context of profound theological and spiritual truth. We need to notice this, because we have a tendency to overlook it.

There's something else we need to notice, too, and it relates to *emphasis*.

Have any of you ever enjoyed a concert by that world-famous one-armed violinist? Probably not—there isn't one. One-armed people can't play the violin.

Have any of you ever been out on a lovely afternoon in the wilderness, looked up into the sky, and seen circling there, effortlessly up in the air currents, a gorgeous, one-winged eagle? Probably not. One-winged eagles can't fly.

I point this out because when you look into Colossians 3:18-21, at first sight you will see four points. Verse 18 speaks to wives ("submit to your husbands"); verse 19 to husbands ("love your wives"); verse 20 to children ("obey your parents"); and verse 21 to fathers ("do not embitter your children").

My congregation at Elmbrook is used to getting three-point sermons. When I came to this passage, no doubt they wondered, "How on earth is he going to get those four points into a three-point sermon?" That poses real problems for people like me.

The answer is that, as I looked at it, it became clear it would be as wrong to teach it as a three-point sermon as it would be to teach it as a four-point sermon. Why? Because there are two couplets of truth here, not four.

The first relates to husbands *and* wives; the second, to

parents *and* children. Never try teaching wives to submit to their husbands apart from admonishing husbands to love their wives. And by the same token, don't try teaching children to obey their parents apart from reminding parents not to embitter their children. The two come together like the arms of a violinist, like the wings of an eagle.

With that in mind, we're almost ready to launch into this section of Scripture. But before we do, let me make one last introductory remark.

About the same time that Paul wrote to the church in Colossae, he also wrote to the church in Ephesus. Geographically these churches were very close together, and they naturally had very close ties because the one was founded from the other. Colossae, if you like, was a daughter church of the church in Ephesus because of the ministry of Epaphras.

What difference does that make to us? Just this. When the apostle wrote to Ephesus, he dealt with the same kinds of things that he handled in Colossae, but in Ephesians he gives a much fuller treatment of the problems. Therefore we can think of Ephesians as a kind of commentary on the epistle to the Colossians, and very often we ought to refer to both of them at the same time. That's particularly true of the passage before us.

In the next few chapters, then, we will often refer to the apostle's own published commentary on Colossians—Ephesians. And to read it you won't even have to make a trip to the bookstore!

Ladies First

*Wives, submit to your husbands, as is fitting
in the Lord.*

If you want to antagonize a lot of women today,
just tell them Paul is a friend of yours.

"Paul who?" they may say.

"The apostle Paul," you will reply, and that will conclude
your part of the conversation. Prepare to be assaulted. Paul does
not do well in feminist circles.

Part of the problem, of course, is that these ladies have not
taken the trouble to study the things Paul said in the context in
which he operated. Their anger stems from uninformed acquain-
tance with statements of his such as "wives, submit to your husbands." All you've got to do is to breathe the word *submit* and
you're in trouble. Quite frankly, a lot of women today aren't into
submission.

But notice something: Neither are men. In fact, it would
be true to say that as a rule of thumb, most people aren't into
submission. Many positively despise it. And yet that doesn't
change the fact that submission is a normal, human experience.
Without submission society cannot survive.

The Bible teaches this very thing. Although God is the One in whom all authority resides, the Scriptures tell us he delegates some of it to human authorities in order that society might flourish. For that delegated authority to function, submission must take place—and if necessary, be enforced. When submission to authority breaks down, society comes apart at the seams.

Some time ago I was invited, much to my surprise, to address a meeting of the police chiefs of Wisconsin. They were holding a convention at a large hotel in downtown Milwaukee, and although I thought it was odd they wanted me to speak to them, I went anyway, thinking it would be interesting. I wanted to hear what I would have to say to them.

We fell behind schedule right away when several of the chiefs sought liquid reinforcement of their ample lunch. They headed straight for the bar and did not want to leave. Eventually we did manage to coax them out, but it was obvious they were in no mood for an immediate after-lunch session. It was, in fact, a particularly poor time to have it, which is probably why they placed me in that slot.

Finally the chairman got up and announced, "We've got the Rev. [I thought, *Oh, no!*] Briscoe here to speak."

I didn't have a very enthusiastic audience before I began; it grew considerably less so when he mentioned the word *reverend*. I got up, thinking, *I'll do what I can with them.*

"You are probably wondering why I am here," I began. "You will be encouraged to know that I, too, am wondering why I am here. But the reason I accepted this surprising invitation to speak to you today is this: We're all in the same business."

That got their attention.

"I, as you know, am a reverend, as your chairman explained to you. And you are police chiefs; reverends and police chiefs are all in the same business."

They were really interested by now, so I explained from Romans chapter 13 why I was saying such a ridiculous thing. God has delegated his authority, I told them, and those who hold authority in government are called "ministers of God." So reverends and police chiefs really are in the same business.

Now, that will change your attitude toward traffic cops.

The next time one stops you, say, "Good morning, minister!" That's a line he will not have heard before. Before he can say too much to you, say, "Have you read Romans 13 recently?" and give an exposition of it. He'll double your fine, but it will be worth it.

The point of all this, of course, is that God has delegated his authority, and this delegated authority requires from all citizens a degree of submission. Remember that when we think in terms of wives submitting to their husbands. Submission is a normal human experience.

But it is more than that. Submission is also a particularly Christian attitude, a peculiar and special Christian disposition. A Christian is a person who acknowledges Jesus Christ as Lord; that's the essence of Christianity. As soon as you say, "Lord," you assume submission.

This strikes at the heart of why many people are not interested in Christianity. It's not that they would not like many of its benefits—they'd be terrifically interested in those. No, they are not too enthusiastic for one basic reason, and it is this: They refuse to submit their lives to the Lordship of Christ.

They won't very often admit that's the reason. In fact, they'll come up with all kinds of arguments and debates and discussions to claim otherwise. But the fundamental, underlying reason they reject Christianity is that they realize it demands they relate to Jesus Christ on the basis of his Lordship.

"Why do you call me 'Lord, Lord,'" Jesus asked on one occasion, "and do not do the things that I say?" It is utter nonsense to live in disobedience to Jesus while still calling him Lord. The essence of relating to Lordship is submissive obedience. And that is the basis upon which Paul gives instructions to husbands and wives.

It's in the context of that same theme that the apostle, in the book of Ephesians, introduces the idea of wives submitting to their husbands. Remember that Ephesians is an amplified statement of what Paul first mentions in Colossians. In Ephesians, Paul wrote, "Submit to one another out of reverence for Christ. Wives, submit to your husbands as to the Lord . . ." (5:21, 22). It is in that setting that we teach submission of the wife to the husband. To divorce it from that context to is do despite to the biblical teaching.

What do we mean, then? What do we mean when we talk about submission as a wife's responsibility?

Notice, first of all, that the idea of the wife's submitting to her husband in Ephesians 5 is a result of Paul's statement that the husband is the head of the wife. He uses a model so they will understand. In the same way that Christ is the head of the body, the church, so the husband is the head of the wife. Therefore, wives, submit to your husband's headship.

Now, as soon as we say *head,* we unfortunately think in terms of "head honcho." That is precisely what gets some women upset about submitting to their husbands. They've got this image of the "head honcho" standing up there immovable, infallible, unapproachable, and unbearable . . . and they're supposed to submit to him?

But to think in terms of the husband as the head and the wife submitting to the head purely in terms of an isolated, authoritarian figure who requires a slavish, unpaid submission from the wife is a total caricature and parody of what Paul says. He's not saying that at all.

Remember the two wings? I wish I could talk about both of them at the same time, but unfortunately I've got to take them one at a time. Bear in mind the "wing" of the husband while we concentrate on this "wing" of the wife. The key here is that the husband is the head of the wife just as Christ is the head of the church. Paul is not thinking only in terms of leadership and response to leadership—although that idea is clearly there—but of a leadership that is deeply concerned to strengthen the relationship, nourishing and cherishing and helping the other to mature.

This idea of the husband as head can be interpreted in a variety of ways. My wife interprets it this way. She says, "Stuart, you are the head of our family. But I am the neck, which means two things: (1) I support you; (2) I help turn you whichever way I wish."

Assuming the husband understands biblical headship, it will not be too difficult for a wife to say, "You know, it's pretty obvious that somebody has to be the leader here. It's best to go along with this leadership, recognizing that it's going to be something I'm growing into more and more myself. This leadership is the resource from which I'm drawing help and encouragement all the time. Therefore it's pointless to buck it or to fight it. I'll join in and live in the good of it."

Notice another thing the apostle says: "Wives, submit to your husbands, as is fitting in the Lord." Paul says submission of wives to husbands is "fitting," appropriate. Why? Because submissive attitudes on everyone's part are essential for society's well-being. Submission on the part of every Christian clearly demonstrates to the world the Lordship of Christ.

Let's summarize what Paul has said thus far. "Wives, submit to your husbands" means, first of all, that submission is normative. Second, submission is something particularly and peculiarly Christian. And third, if the proper functioning of the home requires any more submission, the husband accepts everything that biblical headship demands and the wife gladly responds to that headship. That's basically it.

So far there might not seem to be anything unusual in any of this. But shortly we'll discover that Paul's teaching here is radical indeed.

Big Man and the Little Woman

*Husbands, love your wives and
do not be harsh with them.*

Y ears ago a big, obnoxious fellow, out of control and reeking of drink, was embarrassing everyone around him—especially his beautiful young wife. She was embarrassed to death.

Finally he dragged her over, shoved her in front of me, and said, "I just want to introduce you to my better half."

"She certainly is," I replied, giving him a start. "You're absolutely right, she is your better half, because she is half of you, and you are embarrassing her to death. And as far as I can see, she is infinitely better than you."

A lot of men like Paul's teaching that wives should submit to their husbands. What they somehow forget is the apostle's admonition that husbands must love their wives.

It's time now to look at the other wing on the eagle, to observe the other arm of the violinist. "Husbands, love your wives," Paul says.

Now, the Colossian women were accustomed to submission. Their culture required it. When Paul said, "Wives, submit to your husbands," they no doubt responded, "So what's new? Wives around here have always had to submit to their husbands. We're just pieces of property. Just chattel. Men can get us when they want and they can get rid of us when they please, and that's all there is to it. We've got to submit; we don't have any other option."

But then Paul turned to the husbands, and things quickly got radical.

"Husbands, love your wives," Paul commanded.

"That's it?" you protest. "That's what you mean by 'radical'? I was hoping for something more!"

I admit it doesn't look radical at all to us. But to the men of first century Colossae, it most certainly did. It was one of the most radical statements they had ever heard: "Husbands, love your wives." Colossian men snapped awake when Paul said that. "You've got to be kidding," they sputtered. "What? We don't have to love our wives! You don't love chattel. What do you mean, love our wives?"

It had never occurred to these men that they should love their wives. They never dreamed it was the other wing of the eagle, the second arm of the violinist. It was a radical statement . . . for them as well as for us.

Love, just like submission, is both a norm and a particular Christian attitude. So before I get after the men too much about loving their wives, let's remind ourselves that love makes the world go 'round.

Psychologists tell us that the two most common problems of those with aberrant psychological behavior is their inability to express and to receive love. These unhappy people "short circuit" from lack of love. All human beings are made to love and to be loved.

Ancient Colossae, in the time Paul was writing, suffered from a gross perversion of God-ordained order: Husbands weren't even remotely interested in loving their wives. It just wasn't done.

If I meet someone today and ask, "Are you a normal human being, are you a loving sort of person, do you know how to express love and to receive love?" If that person says no, then I know I've met someone with some problems.

If I meet a Christian and say, "Would you say that God has worked in your life to make you more loving than you were before you became a believer?" and he says no, I worry about that. You know why, don't you? Believers are identified by one thing. They understand they are are to *love* the Lord their God. They know they are to *love* their neighbors as themselves; that *love* is a fruit of the Spirit; that faith, hope, and *love* are going to abide, but the greatest of them all is *love*; that Jesus said "By this shall all men know that you are my disciples, that you *love* one another"; and that we *love* because God first *loved* us.

The dominant theme of Christian experience is love, coupled with submission. It is utter nonsense to talk about healthy spiritual experience divorced from a loving attitude and a submissive spirit. These two things are part and parcel of the Christian walk.

Without going any further, apply that to your marriage. You say you've got problems? You say, "We sure do have problems." Ask yourself if it might really be a spiritual problem. Maybe you've overlooked the fact that submission and love, while they are normative for society, are particularly and uniquely required for Christians. They ought to characterize your Christian experience generally and be brought into sharp focus in your family.

Let's look at how Paul amplifies this in the book of Ephesians. He gives us another model. In the same way that he uses Christ as head of the church to model the husband's headship of his wife, so he describes Christ's love for the church as a model of how a husband ought to love his wife.

> *Husbands, love your wives, just as Christ loved the church and gave himself up for her to make her holy, cleansing her by the washing with water through the word, and to present her to himself as a radiant church, without stain or wrinkle or any other blemish, but holy and blameless. In this same way, husbands ought to love their wives as their own bodies. He who loves his wife loves himself. After all, no one ever hated his own body, but he feeds and cares for it, just as Christ does the church* ... (Ephesians 5:25-29).

Notice Christ's attitude toward the church. Three things come immediately to mind.

Christ loved the church so much he gave himself up for her. Now, everybody is good at being selfish, but it may be that men are better at it than women. We really are quite good at it.

Do you know what best demonstrates the love of a husband for the wife when he—an innately insensitive, selfish creature—begins to understand what it means to unselfishly give up himself for his wife?

Perhaps it's just at this point that some of us are having problems. We don't need a lot of ongoing therapy. What we need is men who will say that love is both a normal human experience and something peculiarly Christian, and who will unselfishly give up themselves for their wives.

We must ask ourselves, "What is it that she wants me to become unselfish about? To be truthful, I guess she *has* told me—and I've called it nagging. Well, I'll stop calling it nagging, and I'll start listening. Maybe she has a point. Maybe she's right. Maybe I could demonstrate my love for her . . . and maybe that would start the other wing flapping. Maybe she wouldn't be on my case all the time. I might even find a sweet little lady around the place. I don't know what I'd do with her, but that would be encouraging."

Do you get the picture? Christ's attitude toward the church—he gave himself up for her.

But that's not all. Christ also cares for her and feeds her. One of the great, legitimate raps on men by women goes something like this: "He doesn't care what I think, he's not interested in how I feel. He's out there doing his own thing, he comes back in when he's good and ready, he demands this, he demands that. He sits down in front of the tube, puts up his feet, and demands, 'Where's my shirt for tomorrow morning?' Then he tells me to keep the kids quiet. Let me tell you, I try to keep the little wretches quiet all day long. I'm glad he's here now to take some of the load, but I wish he'd get off my case. I get enough of that from the kids! I've had it up to here!"

I wonder what would happen if a husband started to love his wife to the extent of becoming unselfish, if he began to care enough about her to be interested in what she thinks and what she feels. What would happen if he would care for her and feed her? That's the expression, right there in Ephesians 5:29.

In other words, when a husband understands what his wife is saying and notices what she's feeling and knows what she's thinking, and then responds to it and accepts his responsibility to nourish and encourage and feed her in that area—that's when real spirituality breaks out and grows. "Husbands, love your wives" is an exceedingly down-to-earth piece of counsel. It's a call to loving action as well as to restraint; don't be harsh with her, don't be hard on her, but do be kind.

Husbands, give up yourselves. Care for and feed your wife.

How should you do this? Paul says you do it by regarding her as you would your own body. In the same way that Christ looks at the church as his body, Paul says the husband and wife are bound to each other . . . and they should look at each other as being part of the one. If husbands would do just this one thing, good marriages would blossom and flourish all over the country.

It seems to me that when wives submit to their husbands and husbands love their wives, we're going to get a balance. There'll be no one-armed violinists, no one-winged eagles.

But what if *your* spouse is a wretch? What if *your* spouse sniffs at Paul's word to husbands and wives? What if . . .

Let me stop you right there. We don't have time to get into all the variations on "what if" right now. Suffice it to say that Paul has laid down the principles, and instead of talking about all the exceptions, let's begin operating on what God has already shown us. Let's start with ourselves and respond to God's working in our hearts by his Spirit.

If we start working on ourselves, we can start worrying about the other person later.

Chips off the Old Block

Children, obey your parents in everything, for this pleases the Lord. Fathers, do not embitter your children, or they will become discouraged.

I remember a time when our eldest child was about one year old. He was staggering around the kitchen, holding on to things to keep himself afloat.

Three racks filled with vegetables sat in one corner, the top rack loaded with ripe tomatoes. I saw him stumble over toward these delicacies and inspect them. A smile crept over his face as he picked up one to look closer. Soon it was no longer in his hand. Splash! It was now on the wall.

"David, do not do that!" I commanded.

He looked at me, all twelve months of him, and picked up a second one.

"Do not do it, do not do it," I repeated.

Splash!

I grabbed his little hand and said, "Don't do it! What you've done is worthy of corporal punishment. You do it again and you'll get some sergeant punishment."

He picked up the next one.

"Don't do it, David, don't you do it. I'll spank you if you do."

Splash!

We were getting low on tomatoes by this time. He therefore decided a slight change of tactics was in order. Do you know what he did? He picked up the fourth tomato, held his other little hand out, and said, "Spank it, Daddy." Then he was ready.

Splash!

I picked him up and announced, "You're going to your room, David." I took him there, stood him on a little chest that made him the same height as I, and gave him a little talking to with my preacher's finger. As my finger came forward the third time, he caught it, stuck it in his mouth, and bit.

At the same time my wife walked in.

"Admit it, you're beaten," she advised.

She was right, unfortunately.

You know, it's hard to teach your kids obedience. That's why we simply give up on it so often ... and why we produce so many little sociopaths. Our society is marked by lack of respect for authority. School teachers complain about it all the time, and they're quitting by the busloads. What a tragedy! Sunday school teachers have had it with these kids, and youth workers complain it's the hardest thing in the world to get these kids to do what they're supposed to do.

What's the problem? The problem is back home!

Bill Cosby explains it in his own inimitable way: "Parents don't want justice; they just want peace and quiet."

He's right.

Rather than dealing with children in a way that firmly yet gently leads them along, we give up. Kids don't bother about being obedient, and ironically, their parents end up embittering and discouraging them.

We observed "two wings" when we talked about husbands and wives, and we see "two wings" again when Paul gives instructions to parents and children. Here they are: "Children, obey your parents" (v. 20); "Fathers, do not embitter your children" (v. 21). (The word *fathers* here is the same word found in Hebrews 11:23

and can mean either *father* or *parents*. For the sake of convenience in this general context, let's assume it is *parents*).

On the one hand, "children, obey your parents," and on the other hand, "parents, don't embitter your children."

The operative word for children here is "obey your parents."

"Do what I say."

"Why?"

"Because I said so."

That's one approach, and it's sometimes valid—particularly when the parent doesn't know why: "I don't know why, but my parents made me do it, so it's your turn now. You can get even later."

Telling someone to obey, like telling someone to submit, often prompts a reaction. And yet obedience is a normal, human experience, just like submission. Sooner or later you'll learn it. April 15 you'll learn it. Drive down the freeway in full view of a little sign that says 55, ignore it, multiply it by two, and keep going—you'll learn it. "Stay away from that fire," you're warned, but you stick your finger in the flame. You'll learn. Go swimming in a lake posted "No Swimming—Dangerous Currents"; you'll learn obedience when they haul you out nine-tenths dead.

Everybody learns obedience. It's a normal, human experience. It's also a special Christian attitude.

Somebody has said, "Man was made with a will; little boys were made with a won't." That's probably true. That's how you discover you've got a will, by exercising your won't. Everyone who has a will has a won't, and whether you will or you won't determines the quality of life you'll enjoy.

Christians understand this and have made their decision. Just as the Lord Jesus Christ said to his Father, "Not my will, but thine be done," the Christian has said to the Lord Jesus, "Not my will, but thine be done."

Christians are people who are uniquely committed to being obedient. That being the case, parents have a special responsibility to the little rascals they bring into the world. It's their job to equip their children to become healthy members of society and mature believers in the Lord, to fit them for earth and for eternity. That's your job as a parent.

Remember that you'll never fit them for earth or for heaven, however, unless you teach them obedience. They have to learn it. Life without discipline is chaos, and discipline has to be learned the hard way.

Unfortunately, many parents have the wrong idea about discipline. They are either unbending in it or negligent with it, and they wind up embittering their children. Paul cautions us against that: "Fathers, do not embitter your children, or they will become discouraged."

There are two equally good ways of embittering your children. You can embitter them by being too strict and by not giving them the freedom to develop. Or you can embitter them by giving so much freedom that they get the feeling you couldn't care less what happens to them. Both methods work equally well.

It seems to me that the best preventative and antidote to those bad attitudes is to remember the Lord, the One to whom those children really belong. You brought them into the world, it's true, but he expects you to work to fit them for earth and for heaven.

To do this it's going to take an awful lot of diligence and perseverance on your part, a lot of obedience on your children's part, and all the resources of which Colossians speaks. There are no shortcuts.

Parents and children—get the two wings flapping. Children, obey your parents! Parents, don't embitter or discourage your children!

If you want a smooth flight, it's the only way.

Working Out

1. Some people refuse to "submit" because they think submission destroys their personal dignity and worth. But the same word translated "submit" in Colossians 3:18 ("wives, *submit* to your husbands") is used in Luke 2:51 to describe Jesus as a boy: "Then he went down to Nazareth with [his parents] and *was obedient* to them." It also occurs in 1 Corinthians 14:32, where Paul says "The spirits of prophets are *subject* to the control of prophets."

    A. When Jesus submitted to his parents in Luke 2:51, do you think Mary and Joseph saw themselves as better than their son? Did his submission weaken their belief that he was the Savior of the world, or strengthen it? What does Jesus' willingness to submit to his parents mean to you?

    B. Does the fact that "prophets" control their gift make their gift any less valuable? Does it demean their gift, or does it allow for an orderly service that helps people and pleases God? (cf. 1 Corinthians 14:40)

2. A great enemy of love in marriage is bitterness. The word translated "harsh" in Colossians 3:19 ("husbands, love your wives and do not be *harsh* with them") means "to be embittered against."

    A. How does bitterness kill love in marriage? Has it infected yours? Are you harboring any grudges toward your spouse which might grow into a full-blown case of bitterness? In what concrete ways have you or your friends gotten rid of bitterness?

    B. What are some practical ways of showing love? Pick one way that's unusual for you and plan a specific day this week to express it.

3. Take a mental trip back in time to your teen-age years. Remember any times when your parents unfairly frustrated you? How did you feel? What did they do to exasperate you?

    Now fast-forward to today. In Colossians 3:21 Paul says parents should be careful not to "embitter" or "irritate" their children so that they become "discouraged" or "lose heart." How are you doing on that score? What do you need to do to avoid irritating your children in the ways your parents might have frustrated you?

Second Wind

1. Ephesians 5:22-6:4.
   In what ways is marriage like Christ's relationship to the church?

2. 1 Peter 3:1-7 cf. Genesis 16, 21.
   Does Sarah's "submission" mean she had no mind of her own?

3. 1 Corinthians 7:3-5.
   How does this passage remind you of the one-winged eagle or the one-armed violinist?

4. Deuteronomy 6.
   How important is it to talk frequently with your children about the things of God?

5. Proverbs 1:8-19; 2:1-11; 3:1-12.
   What specific things does Solomon advise his son about? Might these be good topics for discussion in your family?

What about Work?

Slaves, obey your earthly masters in everything;
and do it, not only when their eye is on you
and to win their favor,
but with sincerity of heart and reverence for the Lord.
Whatever you do, work at it with all your heart,
as working for the Lord, not for men,
since you know that you will receive
an inheritance from the Lord as a reward.
It is the Lord Christ you are serving.
Anyone who does wrong will be repaid for his wrong,
and there is no favoritism.

Masters, provide your slaves with what is right and fair,
because you know that you also have a Master in heaven.
Colossians 3:22-4:1

Hi Ho, Hi Ho!

Y ou can almost hear the seven dwarfs singing as you read the bumper sticker on the car in front of you: "I owe, I owe, so off to work I go!"

Remember, I said "almost." Somewhere along the way, somebody changed the words to the song. And not only the words—they changed the sentiment, too.

Do you remember Disney's version of Snow White and the Seven Dwarfs? The dwarfs were a happy, contented bunch (Grumpy excepted), glad for the opportunity to work. They didn't complain about it (Grumpy excepted)—they whistled while they worked. They worked because they liked to work. Their song was, "Hi ho, hi ho, it's off to work we go!" and they sang it with delight.

Enter the bumper sticker. Gone is the idea of work as joy. Today, people work to pay bills. If they didn't have to pay bills, they wouldn't work. Work isn't a joy for them, it's a curse.

If people whistled while they worked in our society, their co-workers would either question

• their manners ("Ugh! Why doesn't he cut that out?"),

- their morals ("Hmmm. I wonder what *he's* up to?"),

- or their mind ("Yikes! A wacko that likes to work!").

We'd think something was out of kilter somewhere.

The truth is, something *is* out of kilter—but what's fouled up is our negative view of work. It turns out the dwarfs are closer to Paul's teaching on work than many of us are.

Paul sees work as a gift of God. He sees it as an opportunity to revel in God's provision and grace. He wants us to do it gladly, delightedly, as to God himself. He doesn't want us to weasel out as much pay for as little work as possible.

I recently saw a bogus memo supposedly issued by a certain company's administration. The memo was written by one of the staff's more creative members to get a rise out of her co-workers.

She was successful.

Here's what the memo said:

To: All staff
From: Administration
Re: Personal phone calls

Because of the increasing number of staff who are using business phones for personal phone calls and tying up available phone lines in non-productive activity, we have laid down the following telephone rules:

1. All telephone calls will be monitored from a central switchboard location. We will be hiring a full-time person to do this. If the call is a personal one, the duration and cost of the call will be recorded, and the cost of the phone call and the employee's time will be deducted from the employee's paycheck.

2. Each time an employee is found to be making a personal call on company time, a letter of warning will be sent to the employee. A duplicate letter will be placed in the employee's permanent records. Accumulation of three letters of warning will result in a fine to the employee. The fine will consist of either $25 (deducted from the employee's paycheck) or 8 hours of manual labor in the warehouse. Employees delinquent more than 60 days in paying their fines will be dismissed.

We encourage all employees to make their personal phone calls on their breaks and lunch hours, and to use the pay phone on the corner.

Thank you for your cooperation.

The memo was greeted by a howl of protest, with especially outraged shrieks from one young man. He was about to march over to administration to protest when the perpetrator kindly informed him of her deceit. He'd been hoodwinked.

Sheepishly he retreated to his office. He hated to be taken in. But the memo made him think: Why had he swallowed it so easily? Why did he react so strongly? Was it because he had, in fact, been spending too much company time on personal affairs?

He saved the memo as a reminder. You see, the young man is a Christian, and he knows better than to treat work spitefully. When he goes to work, he doesn't really work for his company—he works for his God.

You know what? So does every Christian on the face of the planet. Including me. Including you.

If that's true, then let's work for him heartily, gladly, with gusto. Nobody pays better, and the side benefits are out of this world. Literally.

Off to Work We Go

*Slaves, obey your earthly masters in
everything. . . . Masters, provide your slaves with
what is right and fair.*

o you remember the world-famous, one-armed violinist I told you about a few chapters ago? I asked a congregation once if they had heard of him, and one little old lady put up her hand. When she realized she'd been had, she tried to look as if it weren't her hand.

I do apologize to her. You cannot play a violin with one arm. And neither can a one-winged eagle fly. Paul doesn't tell wives to submit to their husbands without telling husbands to love their wives. He doesn't tell children to obey their parents without telling parents not to embitter their children.

By the same token, Paul does not tell slaves to obey their masters without telling masters to provide their slaves with what is right and fair. Mutuality is the key.

When we find ourselves in the work situation, constantly bear in mind that we are working toward a Christian ethic that acknowledges the true master. Because of how we view each other before the Lord, we are totally committed to generating feelings of mutuality.

By all means, workers obey. By all means, masters provide.

What about Work?

Employees, what is the best way for you to begin to please your boss? I suggest by doing your work, and doing it well. There is nothing new about this. In fact, there is an old saying—not quite as old as the Bible, but better known—which says, "An honest day's pay for an honest day's work." It's a good, old-fashioned idea, and it's thoroughly biblical.

Employers, what is the best way of getting employees to respond to what you want them to do? I suggest it is by looking after them well, by caring for them properly, by showing that you are interested in them as people, and by encouraging and helping and developing them. The best way to ensure that your workers do well for you is to provide for them what is right and fair.

That's the Bible's idea of mutuality.

Unfortunately, this idea of mutuality in the workplace is often turned inside out. It becomes, "How much can I get out of that fat cat, and how little do I need to do for him?" on one side, and "How little do I need to give that guy in order to squeeze the last drop of production out of him?" on the other.

What a heinous thing this is! How far removed from biblical teaching! Biblical teaching says that when we go into the work place, it's a matter of the Master and a matter of mutuality. It makes no difference if you're an employer or an employee.

This idea of doing what is right and good extends to methods of working. "Slaves, obey your earthly masters in everything; and do it, not only when their eye is on you and to win their favor, but with sincerity of heart and reverence for the Lord," Paul writes.

Notice the unusual expression, "not only when their eye is on you." The Greek word here is one that Paul perhaps made up himself. Translated literally, it means "eye service." If you are an employer, do you feel that you need to keep your eye on people all the time to make sure they produce? Or are you in a situation where you honestly know it doesn't matter whether you are there or not, that you can count on your employees to be thoroughly reliable?

If you are employing Christians, let me tell you something. You have every right to expect those believers to produce whether you are there or not. And if you are a believer, you ought to expect to work as hard whether you're being watched or not.

I don't have to tell you that most people today consider this strange thinking. It's different from the norm. But it's thoroughly Christian.

In one factory, a suggestion box was installed for people to contribute ideas designed to improve working conditions. The first suggestion requested that the foreman no longer wear rubber heels on his shoes. They wanted to hear him coming.

That well-known theologian, Groucho Marx, said, "No man leaves before his time—unless, of course, the boss has gone home early."

The common attitude today is to to do one standard of work if your boss is watching, and another if he isn't. Paul specifically addresses this, and says Christians cannot be mere men-pleasers. Eye-service isn't their method. They are not to do the minimum required to keep the boss happy.

Someone has said that those who do not come to work on Mondays are not always sick, they are in a weekend condition. Someone else has said that the number of unemployed is considerably less than the number of those not working.

We must ask ourselves, "Where does the Christian fit into all this?" The answer is easy.

The Christian has a master in heaven. The Christian works as unto the Lord. The Christian is not working because someone's eye is upon him; neither is he just working as a man-pleaser. He has a higher, nobler calling than that. What is the nature of that calling?

He believes that work is a gift from God. He does not get his theology from the Fall, where work has become onerous and a curse. He gets his theology from creation, where he sees that God himself worked, and that he designed man and woman to work together.

The Christian not only sees he was created to work, he sees God incarnate in the person of Christ, working in Nazareth for thirty years. He recognizes that God has given him skills and time and energy, and that if he is to live fulfilled as a person and truly glorify God, he will use his skill and his time and his energy well. In so doing he will become a complete person, and in becoming a complete person will demonstrate how wonderfully God has worked in his life.

In other words, our attitude toward work is not the eye-service and man-pleaser variety, but we see work as a gracious calling, and we do it with joy.

Work = joy. Does it seem like a strange equation to you? Then perhaps it's time you brushed up on the mathematical tables of heaven. Ask the teacher, Jesus, for some help. I'm sure he'll be glad to assist you.

I'm also sure he'll give you some homework.

Thank God—It's Monday!

*Slaves, obey your earthly masters . . . with
sincerity of heart and reverence for the Lord.
Whatever you do, work at it with all your heart,
as working for the Lord, not for men, since you
know that you will receive an inheritance from
the Lord as a reward. It is the Lord Christ you
are serving. Anyone who does wrong will be
repaid for his wrong, and there is no favoritism.*

What a lovely thing a young woman in our church
said to me one Sunday morning. She told me that
when she arrives in the morning to teach her Sunday school class,
she tries to think of the Lord Jesus Christ sitting there in the
back row. It completely changes her attitude to her lesson and
toward her kids.

Believe me, that will do it!

This is exactly what Paul has in mind in this passage of
Scripture. He says that the proper motivation for my work is not
material gain, but something deeply spiritual.

He says Christian workers are to work sincerely and not
with devious motivations. We are to work out of sincerity of heart.
There is to be a spiritual dimension to work; we should work with
reverence for the Lord.

Paul doesn't stop there. He also says Christians are to work
"wholeheartedly." Whatever you do, he says, work at it with all
your heart, wholeheartedly and not halfheartedly, and with
eternal rather than merely temporal things in mind. Why? Not
just because it's right (although it is); but because there will be
a reward.

Even for slaves in difficult circumstances, Paul promises an eternal reward for diligent work. He reminds the master that there are no favorites with God, and that those who misbehave will be treated accordingly. There are eternal ramifications to work.

Now let's put this all together.

Christians who go to work do so sincerely, not deviously. They have a spiritual rather than a material orientation. They work wholeheartedly rather than half-heartedly, and they think eternally rather than temporally.

I was talking to a group of pastors one day about all the problems and frustrations of the pastorate. They talked about about all of the men they knew who were quitting.

One of them said, "In the end, they can't pay you enough for this job. The only reason anybody would ever do it would be out of a sense of calling."

I'd like to think that was true of every Christian. I would like to think that in your workplace you are putting out so prodigiously that they couldn't pay you enough for it—and that's not why you are there, anyway. You are there because of a sense of calling.

Have you ever thought about your job in that way? When you get up in the morning to brush your teeth and get ready for work, do you think, "Wow, God has called me to this job. I wonder what he'll ask me to do today?"

A job is not just a job. God has put you where he has for reasons that he may not reveal, but for reasons which apparently please him. As long as he keeps you there, make sure that you honor his call. When you do, you'll not only become a valuable showpiece of God's grace in your workplace, but you'll experience the peace and contentment that God showers on those who honor him. That's a call to get excited about!

Those who want to develop such an excitement about their call need to add one more thing to their portfolio, Paul says. Maturity is a necessary dimension of the working Christian's attitude.

Twice in Colossians 3:22-4:1 Paul speaks of what his readers already know. "Slaves, since you *know* that you will receive an inheritance from the Lord ... Masters, because you *know* that you have a Master in heaven."

What's he saying? He's saying that in back of their work habits is good theology. In fact, that's the theme of Colossians.

Paul's readers needed to square away their theology. They needed to understand who Christ is, to know how they were related to him. The apostle was convinced that a thorough knowledge of these things would get them excited about what it meant to be raised with Christ, to have died to the old life, to walk in a newness of life, to serve the Lord Christ.

Whether they were in the church or in the family or in the marketplace, what would happen if they took to heart the words of God? Paul says they would be a distinctive people.

Nothing has changed since then.

One of the great things we should look forward to is for Christian men and women, boys and girls, to do their work as unto the Lord.

All you need to do is to ask yourself a question: "What is the difference in my work attitude between Monday morning and Friday afternoon?"

If there is a distinguishable difference, you're probably missing the point. If you start work on Monday morning with leaden feet and a heavy heart and grumbles at your lips, and if you've adopted the prevailing "Thank God, it's Friday" mentality, something's amiss. What does that say about serving the Lord Christ? If we succumb to the prevailing attitude about work, what does that do to Paul's admonition that "Whatever you do, do it heartily, as unto the Lord"?

One of the great places in which we get the chance to live out our Christianity is in the marketplace. Let's not blow it! It's too great and exciting a privilege, and we've been commissioned by too great and wonderful a Lord.

The Master's Voice

*Slaves, obey your earthly masters in everything;
and do it, not only when their eye is on you and
to win their favor, but with sincerity of heart and
reverence for the Lord. Whatever you do, work at
it with all your heart, as working for the Lord,
not for men, since you know that you will receive
an inheritance from the Lord as a reward. It is
the Lord Christ you are serving. Anyone who does
wrong will be repaid for his wrong, and there is
no favoritism.*

*Masters, provide your slaves with what is right
and fair, because you know that you also have a
Master in heaven.*

It's common for us preachers to say that the Christian faith is the most liberating force in the universe. We say it frees men and women from the shackles of sin and brings them into the glorious freedom of the gospel.

But skeptics often have an objection to all this talk of freedom and liberation: If it's true, how come the Bible never condemns slavery? If "freedom" and "liberation" are such important biblical themes, why did it take until the nineteenth century to make slavery illegal in such "Christian" countries as England and the United States of America?

It's a good question. And although I'm sure I don't know all the reasons, I think I know at least part of the answer.

Did you know that slaves accounted for more than half of the population of the Roman Empire at the time Paul wrote his letters? What do you think would have happened to those slaves if someone at that time had been able to abolish slavery? What would have happened to the millions of people who would be released, all of whom lacked any means of supporting themselves?

I think that is why Paul doesn't tackle the slavery problem head-on. The church wasn't strong enough. It couldn't have coped with the waves of destitute former slaves, and it's certain the government of the time wouldn't have lifted a finger to help. Condemning slavery apparently wasn't the way to go, and so Paul does not condone slavery or condemn it, but rather confronts it. Notice the key here—he confronts it in terms of attitude. He confronts it in terms of work ethic.

I want you to notice something that is slightly below the surface of this passage. The Greek word for "Lord" is *kyrios. Kyrios* can also be translated "master." Paul riddled this passage of Scripture with the word *kyrios* in order to make a play on the words "Lord" and "master." Let me give the passage again, this time using the Greek word instead of the English translation.

> *Slaves, obey your earthly* kyrios *in everything, and do it not only when their eye is on you and to win their favor, but with sincerity of heart and reverence for the* kyrios. *Whatever you do, work at it with all your heart, as working for the* kyrios *and not for men, since you know that you will receive an inheritance from the* kyrios *as a reward. It is the* kyrios *Christ you are serving. Anyone who does wrong will be repaid for his wrong, and there is no favoritism. Kyrioi, provide your slaves with what is right and fair, because you know that you also have a* kyrios *in heaven.*

Do you see the dominant theme of Paul's message? The dominant theme is lordship.

What makes all the difference to believers everywhere is that Jesus Christ is their Lord. If Jesus Christ is your Lord, whether you are a slave or a freeman is of secondary importance. What is of primary importance is that you live in your socioeconomic situation as unto the Lord.

For Paul's day, this teaching was radical in the extreme.

It's not a great deal less radical today. Why? Let me give an example.

When we find ourselves in difficult circumstances in the marketplace, what is our usual tendency? Our normal response is to try to change the circumstances.

But Paul says, "No. When Christians find themselves in difficult circumstances in the marketplace, they don't immediately change their circumstances. They change their attitude."

A young lady came up to me after one Sunday service when I spoke on this passage and said, "When I saw what you were going to be teaching this morning, I was dreading it, absolutely dreading it. But fortunately something has happened to me recently that changed things so I could handle it."

"What happened?" I asked.

"For five long years I detested my job," she said. "I wanted to do all that I could to get out of it. I wanted to do all that I could to change it. I wanted to do all that I could just to escape from the whole thing. Then one day I decided I was going to go back to work and acknowledge the Lord Jesus as my Master in my own work situation. My circumstances haven't changed—I have. And believe it or not, I want to stay in my job because I am a new person."

That is exactly what Paul is teaching.

Am I an employer or an employee? That is not the important question, according to Paul. The important question is, "Who is my master?"

What is the relationship between me and my employer, between me and my employees? That is not the important question, according to Paul. The important question is, Who is my Master?

When I get up on a Monday morning and get in the car to drive to work, what is my mental attitude?

The answer, if I am Christian, is this: "I serve the Lord Christ." That is the attitude which must shape our week's work.

If I am an employee, my reaction to those in authority over me will demonstrate my attitude to authority in general, and particularly as it is delegated from the ultimate authority, the Lord Jesus.

If I am an employer, always I bear in mind that as I exercise authority over my employees, I have one in authority over me—the same Lord Jesus.

Therefore, whether I am an employer or an employee, what

must I remember? I must remember who is my master.

The RCA company used to have as its trade symbol a dog staring at a phonograph, accompanied by the words, "His master's voice." I never saw the dog do a thing but sit there, but from the way he was sitting I'll bet anything he'd jump if his master's voice said, "Jump!"

Who is *our* master? The Lord Jesus. In Colossians 3:22-4:1 he's telling us to jump—not out of fear or mere duty, but because he is the sort of loving master who rewards faithful service.

Remember that the next time you go to work, and chances are that soon you'll be looking at your job in a whole new way. Your circumstances may not change, but you will—and you'll have one mighty pleased Lord in heaven.

I've no doubt he'll tell you about it some day!

Working Out

1. Paul supplies both a positive and a negative motivation for doing hard, honest work in verses 24-25.

The positive motivation is one of reward. Work hard, Paul says, "since you know that you will receive an inheritance from the Lord as a reward." The Greek phrase translated "an inheritance" is definite—it literally reads "*the* reward of *the* inheritance." Paul probably has in mind here the same thing he spoke of in Romans 8:17: "Now if we are children [of God], then we are *heirs— heirs* of God and *co-heirs* with Christ . . ." So the question is, "If we are co-heirs with Christ—if his inheritance is our inheritance— what does Christ inherit?" The answer is in Hebrews 1:2, where the writer says Christ has been "appointed *heir of all things.*"

A. Why should knowing that believers are to inherit "all things" through Christ be a motivation to work hard? Does it motivate you? Why or why not?

B. Notice that the reward promised for faithful work on earth is an inheritance that can't be claimed until our earthly lives are completed. Is this an encouragement to you or a disappointment? Why? Does concentrating on heaven and its pleasures help you keep perspective on the disappointments you may face in your job? (See Romans 8:18-25)

The negative motivation is one of discipline: "anyone who does wrong will be repaid for his wrong, and there is no favoritism." Remember that this passage is directed toward *Christians*—Paul expects that good service is rewarded and disobedience is disciplined. He said the same thing in 2 Corinthians 5:10: "For *we* must *all* appear before the judgment seat of Christ, that *each one* may receive what is due him for the things done *while in the body,* whether good or bad," where the context makes it crystal clear he is talking to believers.

A. Does knowing that you will one day stand before Christ at his judgment seat give you hope or fright? Why? Do any of your work habits need to change?

B. Notice that this judgment isn't until our earthly lives are completed. Does that make it seem less real to you? How can we help each other to remember that it is, in fact, very real?

Second Wind

1. Proverbs 10:4, 5
   What two reasons do these verses give for working hard at your job?

2. 1 Thessalonians 4:11-12
   What bearing do good work habits have on effective evangelism?

3. 2 Thessalonians 3:6-15
   Identify at least four commands that Paul gives believers regarding their work.

4. 1 Timothy 6:1-2
   What ought to be the special relationship between a believing employee and a Christian employer?

5. James 5:1-6
   What is the special danger that successful business people must beware? How should they treat their employees?

IV
Christian Ministries

Assisting Team Members

How Can I Get Involved?

All over the world
this gospel is producing fruit and growing,
just as it has been doing among you
since the day you heard it and understood God's grace
in all its truth.
You learned it from Epaphras, our dear fellow servant,
who is a faithful minister of Christ on our behalf,
and who also told us of your love in the Spirit.
Colossians 1:6-8

I want you to know how much I am struggling for you
and for those at Laodicea,
and for all who have not met me personally.
My purpose is that they may be encouraged in heart
and united in love,
so that they may have the full riches of complete understanding . . .
Colossians 2:1, 2

Devote yourselves to prayer, being watchful and thankful.
And pray for us, too, that God may open a door for our message,
so that we may proclaim the mystery of Christ,
for which I am in chains.
Pray that I may proclaim it clearly, as I should.
Be wise in the way you act toward outsiders;
make the most of every opportunity.
Let your conversation be always full of grace,
seasoned with salt,
so that you may know how to answer everyone.
Colossians 4:2-6

Epaphras, who is one of you and a servant of Christ Jesus,
sends greetings.
He is always wrestling in prayer for you,
that you may stand firm in all the will of God,
mature and fully assured.
Colossians 4:12

You Can Do It!

Several years ago racial strife erupted in Boston over court-ordered school busing. The Boston Marathon was scheduled to take place while this strife was at its peak, and authorities considered canceling the race because part of the course ran through one of the city's most troubled areas. At last they decided to hold it as scheduled in the hope that it might bring people together.

One part of the course features a torturous stretch known as "Heartbreak Hill." Sadists that we are, that's where thousands of spectators gather. They love to see people struggling against Heartbreak Hill. They stand and yell and shout as they see the heaving chests of weary runners about to collapse.

"Come on, 769, you can make it!"

"What's the matter with you? Don't let that old fellow beat you there!"

"Come on, man! Get your act together!"

Now, most of the people shouting are fifty-five pounds overweight and probably couldn't run up a bill, let alone Heartbreak

Hill. But that doesn't stop them from "encouraging."

On this day one young man had "hit the wall" as he approached the foot of Heartbreak Hill. It was highly doubtful he could go a step further. Spectators were yelling at him and shouting at him, "Come on, man, you can make it!" It wasn't helping at all.

In the middle of all this an older man, who was obviously in better shape than the younger runner, came alongside, put his arm around him, put his hip under the young man's hip, and spoke quietly to him. Together, step by step, slowly, painstakingly, they made their way up Heartbreak Hill.

The unusually poignant thing about it was that the young man was black and the older man was white. What a powerful illustration of how to handle racial strife! Just get together, start to carry the burden of another, and encourage each other.

The ministry of encouragement is one of the most significant and important ministries, and yet people often don't recognize it as such. I don't think you have to be particularly gifted to be an encourager. I've got a feeling that anyone who really tries can be an encouragement in one way or another to someone else. Although the ministry of encouragement is one of the most necessary, too often it is the one in which we are least apt to involve ourselves. I don't know anybody who couldn't encourage, and I don't know anyone who couldn't use some encouragement.

But first we need to be clear what we mean by encouragement. The Greek word Paul uses, *parakaleo*, is made up of two words. *Para* means "alongside." A *para*medic is someone who works alongside a medical person. A *para*church organization works alongside a local church. *Kaleo* means "to call." The idea in the Greek, then, is "to call alongside."

This idea translates into English in a number of ways. Sometimes it appears as "beseech," sometimes "exhort," sometimes "comfort," and at other times "encourage." The idea is always that one person comes alongside another, sharing whatever it is that they need to be helped along the way.

Everybody can do that, and everybody needs that done to them in one way or another.

That's what is needed in society in general and in the church of Jesus Christ in particular. We need people who will take the trouble to get alongside, rather than those who will stand on the sidelines shouting, "Come on, man, what's the matter with you? You can do it!"

We need people who are encouragers. In fact, Paul gives that as the specific reason he sent his friend Tychicus to the Colossians: "I am sending him to you for the express purpose that you may know about our circumstances and that he may *encourage* your hearts" (4:8).

I submit to you that all of us need to examine ourselves very carefully to see how we stack up in the encouragement department. Am I taking the time to encourage others? Do I allow others to encourage me?

Come alongside someone today! You can't provide any better or more valuable medicine anywhere on earth. And all it costs is your time.

An Ounce of Encouragement

I want you to know how much I am struggling for you and for those at Laodicea, and for all who have not met me personally. My purpose is that they may be encouraged in heart ...

Howard Hendricks says he owes his ministry to people who encouraged him.

He came from a poor home where his parents had split up before he was born. On his first day in the fifth grade, his teacher said, "Oh—Howard Hendricks. I've heard a lot about you. I understand you're the worst kid in this school." Challenged like that, Hendricks made sure she was right. Before the year was up he'd been gagged, tied to his chair, and punished in countless other ways.

When the next school year rolled around, Hendricks was ready. He wasn't surprised when his sixth grade teacher heard his name and said, "Oh, so you're Howard Hendricks. I've heard you're the worst boy in this school."

Hendricks thought, *Here we go again.*

But then she continued: "And you know what? I don't believe a word of it."

Throughout the next year she did everything she could to encourage the boy. She praised his work. She helped him when needed. She believed in him. And Hendricks credits her with changing his life forever.

That's what encouragement can do.

Paul knew that. He knew that encouragement inspires people. He knew that if you take the time to encourage people, you can give them new strength, new desire.

Notice how he inspired the Colossians in this passage. First he talks about the concern he has for them. "I want you to know how much I am struggling for you," he writes.

The word "struggling" comes from the arena. It's the word the Greeks used for wrestling. That's how concerned Paul was for these people—he "wrestled" for them.

How did he do it? He doesn't say, but I'll bet he's talking about prayer. That's how he could wrestle and agonize for somebody who was hundreds of miles away.

Let me make a suggestion. Every believer can show an interest in others by taking their burdens in prayer, by committing themselves to sharing the load. One of the most encouraging things you can ever do for people is to commit yourself to pray for them, and then let them know you do it.

It's one thing to pray for people you know. It's another thing to exert yourself for those you've never met. Yet that is exactly what Paul says he was doing for these Colossians.

It's doubtful that Paul ever visited Colossae or Laodicea or any of the churches of the Lycus Valley. He didn't plant the churches there. His students did, one of whom was Epaphras. Paul hadn't even seen the church in Colossae, but that didn't stop him from having a tremendous concern for them and taking time out to pray earnestly for them.

It's possible for Christians to be so wrapped up in their own concerns that they show little care for anyone else. They ignore people outside their immediate universe.

Paul has something to tell us. He says that even though he had never seen these people, even though he was separated from them by hundreds of miles, and even though it was almost certain he'd never meet them, yet he wanted to encourage them by making contact and by expressing his concern for them.

Christian missionaries today are spread out over the face of the whole earth. They have sensed God's call to go hundreds and thousands of miles away from their homelands. They have gone to people whom they had never met. They were not willing to stand on the sidelines as cheerleaders and say, "Come on, you guys in Ethiopia, you can make it!" They got alongside them, put their arms around them, and went with them on the way.

"Now, hold it a minute, Stuart," you say. "Are you telling me that if I'm going to have a ministry of encouragement, I've got to be a missionary?"

No, I'm not saying that at all. If everyone goes off to be a missionary, who'll be left to read my books? No, I'm saying that even though God calls some to go abroad, that doesn't mean the rest of us can stand on the sidelines. I mean that all of us should find at least one way in which we can make contact with people we have never seen, that we find one way to express concern for those we've never met.

Let me put it simply. I'm convinced every believer needs to have a ministry of encouragement to people hundreds and thousands of miles away, whose faces they have never seen.

God doesn't want everybody to go. But I believe it's a realistic assumption that he would like everybody to struggle in prayer for other areas of the body of Christ.

The contact you have with them doesn't have to be anything big. It could be a note, a call, an airletter. It can be something that simply expresses your concern for them and reminds them that you are honestly, genuinely praying for them.

Notice that Paul went out of his way to let the Colossians know about his concern. He could have prayed and not said anything. He didn't have to advertise it, did he? But he chose to let them know. In fact, he starts off the chapter by saying, "I want you to know how much I am struggling for you."

I've been out on mission fields all over the world. I've often sat down and talked with missionaries, many of them in very lonely places. It's been fascinating to note how much they speak about the importance of hearing from people concerned for their welfare. How often they speak to me of the importance of having regular contact with people they have never met who are honestly, genuinely concerned for them!

I'm fairly well known among the missionaries sponsored by my church for writing regularly and briefly. I like to write regularly and briefly. When I get a prayer letter from someone, I don't just look at it and trash it. When I get a prayer letter, I look at it, read it, pray immediately about it, underline something in it, and write a paragraph to them, no more. I'll tell you why.

Many people write pages and pages to me, and as soon as I see a letter pages long, I react. So I think, *Why should I inflict on others what I hate having inflicted on me?*

I firmly believe that every Christian should have contact with, concern for, and communication with someone they have never seen. If you have never done that, think seriously about why you haven't. If you recognize that you haven't but probably should, take steps now—even little steps—to rectify it so that you, too, can be an encouragement to someone else.

Paul inspires the Colossians not only by taking time to remember them, but also by what he says. He gives them commendation, and nothing encourages people more than to be commended for something well done.

Americans are far better at this than the British. Englishmen don't bother to give compliments; Americans are great at it. When you come from Britain to America, you don't know what to do with all the compliments. One old, seasoned British traveler who was well-acquainted with America told me when I first arrived, "The main thing is to ignore most of their compliments. If you start believing them, you'll get such a big head that you'll be useless to God and to man."

I think there is some good advice there, because often the compliments are very shallow indeed. But there is a real place for commendation, and how encouraging it is when we can commend people for things well done.

Look at Colossians 2:5. Paul has heard that the Colossians are orderly in their faith and standing firm in Christ. And he says he's "delighted." That's the word—"delighted."

If you keep in contact with people whom you have never seen, having a desire to encourage them, then they will begin to communicate to you. And when you hear their message, if you've got a heart for the work of God, you will be genuinely delighted in their progress. You'll write back and be unstinting in your commendation. You'll delight to see how orderly and how firm is their faith in Christ.

Those words "orderly" and "firm," by the way, don't come from the arena as did the word "struggling." They come from the military. Paul says the church in Colossae is like a group of soldiers who are standing firm, maintaining their position. They are under fire, but they're not breaking ranks.

Some Christian churches today are out in the boonies, far out of sight, and are under the gun. But they're standing firm. They are orderly, marching on.

What a wonderful thing it would be if you could find out about them, make contact with them, show them your concern, and thereby **en**courage and inspire them in the Lord.

If the church really is the body of Christ, then one part of the body cannot say to the other, "I don't need you." The church in Poland cannot say to the church in America, "I don't need you." The suffering church in Ethiopia has every right to say to the church in America, "We really need you now!"

What a wonderful thing it would be if the church in America were so alert to current events, so interested and concerned, that it would communicate with its Ethiopian brothers, struggle with them, and encourage them in prayer.

I can't imagine that there is one single believer anywhere who could not be involved in that kind of ministry. And I know there is not one single believer anywhere who would not be encouraged by such a ministry.

With that much need and that much opportunity, let's make it our ambition to get started right away.

Keep Looking Up

Devote yourselves to prayer . . .

Many children are convinced that adults give orders solely for the sake of giving orders.

"Do the dishes, won't you honey?" mom asks.

Why? the child thinks. *They're only going to get dirty again later. She just wants to bug me. It's not fair!*

"It looks like it's time to mow the lawn," dad says.

Why? I like long grass. It's natural. He just wants to bug me. It's not fair!

"Clean out your lockers!" the principal orders.

Why? Mold is great! If I want old lunches fossilizing in the bottom of my locker, what is that to him? He just wants to bug me! It's not fair!

Children inevitably grow up, but sometimes they don't grow out of certain patterns of thinking. When given a command later in life, they think it's issued just to bug them. They never see the reason behind the command.

This happens even with Christians. Take Paul's instruction to pray, for example. Some of us chafe under the command, seeing it as one more dull, burdensome responsibility. To be sure, we'd never call it that—we'll smilingly call it "our Christian privilege" and do our best to forget it. We'll get ourselves busy with loads of other things so we won't be bothered.

What a tragedy!

When Paul told the believers at Colossae that they should pray, he was telling them it was absolutely necessary to make sure they had the correct orientation. When you pray, you pray to God Almighty, the Creator of the universe. You get yourself oriented to the center of all things.

If you are oriented toward your society, then your life will be governed by that orientation. If you think in terms of relationships and societal ills and societal opportunities, you will major on your society.

You can be oriented toward yourself. You can be inward-looking, concerned primarily or even exclusively with your own well-being. If that's the case, it's hard for you to see further than the end of your nose.

Or you can be oriented toward heaven. You can have your mind and your heart set on Christ, who is seated at the Father's right hand. That's the Christian orientation as Paul sees it.

It's not that Paul is disinterested in society or uncaring about the individual. Clearly he is interested in both. But neither of these orientations should take precedence over that basic, fundamental orientation of the Christian, which is to set his or her mind and affections on things above, where Christ is seated at the right hand of God.

This is the theme of the passage before us. "Devote yourselves to prayer," Paul writes.

In effect, what he is saying is that we must make sure our orientation is toward the Lord, with particular reference to the risen Christ seated at the Father's right hand. One of the best ways of demonstrating that orientation, quite frankly, will be to become a man or woman of prayer. "Keep looking up," Paul tells us.

Now, I'm the first to admit that my prayer life is not what it should be. I suspect I'm not alone. Many of us probably struggle in this area of prayer. And yet what Paul says here is very straightforward indeed. He insists that people who want to live rightly before the Lord must be men and women of prayer.

But why prayer? What is it about prayer that directs our attention to heaven? Why pray?

The reason is that prayer is a dynamic. Paul asks these people to pray because he believes that prayer makes an impact. He doesn't just ask them to pray so that they will feel good. He doesn't just tell them to pray because it's the sort of thing that religious people do. He requires them to pray because it is effectual, it achieves something; prayer is an exceedingly powerful dynamic.

John Piper spoke of this in his book, *Desiring God*:

> Prayer is the open admission that without Christ we can do nothing. And prayer is the turning away from ourselves to God in the confidence that he will provide the help we need. Prayer humbles us as needy, and exalts God as wealthy. . . . There is a direct correlation between not knowing Jesus well and not asking much from him. A failure in our prayer life is generally a failure to know Jesus. A prayerless Christian is like a bus driver trying alone to push his bus out of a rut because he doesn't know Clark Kent is on board. A prayerless Christian is like having your room wallpapered with Sak's Fifth Avenue gift certificates but always shopping at Ragstock because you can't read.[1]

Unless God works in and through his people, nothing of any lasting value will take place. Unless God intervenes, our efforts will amount to nothing. Unless God intervenes in all our work, there will be nothing of eternal consequence.

But we must be careful that our praying is not designed to surround ourselves with the latest luxuries. Paul asked his friends at Colossae to pray because he needed help in accomplishing the task God had given him. Our prayers are less than exemplary if we concentrate primarily on our own comfort. Listen to Piper once again:

> Isn't it plain that the purpose of prayer is to accomplish a mission? A mission of love—"This I command you, to love one another." It is as though the field commander

(Jesus) called in the troops, gave them a crucial mission (go and bear fruit), handed each of them a personal transmitter coded to the frequency of the general's headquarters, and said, "Comrades, the general has a mission for you. He aims to see it accomplished. And to that end he has authorized me to give each of you personal access to him through these transmitters. If you stay true to his mission and seek his victory first, he will always be as close as your transmitter, to give tactical advice and to send in air cover when you need it."

Could it be that many of our problems with prayer and much of our weakness in prayer come from the fact that we are not all on active duty, and yet we still try to use the transmitter? We have taken a wartime walkie-talkie and tried to turn it into a civilian intercom to call the servants for another cushion in the den.[2]

Prayer is a dynamic, a weapon in battle—but like any weapon, it is utterly useless unless someone takes it up and actually uses it. That is our problem in the church today: We have too few soldiers on active duty.

The question is, why? If prayer is as effective and mighty as Paul seems to think, why don't we engage in it more often? Why don't I? I think Piper is on to something in the passage that follows. See if you think he is, too.

Unless I'm badly mistaken, one of the main reasons so many of God's children don't have a significant life of prayer is not so much that we don't want to, but that we don't plan to. If you want to take a four-week vacation, you don't just get up one summer morning and say, "Hey, let's go today!" You won't have anything ready. You won't know where to go. Nothing has been planned.

But that is how many of us treat prayer. We get up day after day and realize that significant times of prayer should be part of our life, but nothing's ever ready. We don't know where to go. Nothing has been planned. No time. No place. No procedure. And we all know that the opposite of planning is not a wonderful flow of deep, spontaneous experiences in prayer. The opposite of planning is the rut. If you don't plan a vacation you will probably stay home and watch TV. The natural, unplanned flow of spiritual life sinks to the lowest ebb of vitality. There is a race to be run and a fight to be fought. If you want renewal in your life of prayer you must *plan* to see it.

Therefore, my simple exhortation is this: Let us take time this very day to rethink our priorities and how prayer fits in. Make some new resolve. Try some new venture with God. Set a time. Set a place. Choose a portion of Scripture to guide you. Don't be tyrannized by the press of busy days. We all need mid-course corrections. Make this a day of turning to prayer—for the glory of God and for the fullness of your joy.[3]

Amen!

1. John Piper, *Desiring God* (Portland, Ore.: Multnomah Press, 1986), p. 133.
2. Ibid., p. 146.
3. Ibid., pp. 150, 151.

Praying with One Eye Open

Devote yourselves to prayer,
being watchful ...

T he most rewarding things in life usually take discipline. If you hope to lose weight, you discipline your eating habits. If you hope to lead your team in scoring, you discipline yourself with a training schedule. If you hope to play the piano in Carnegie Hall, you discipline your practice times.

Prayer is no different. It is a discipline. I assure you that unless you build some discipline into your life, either prayer will not get started or it won't keep going.

Many people find prayer boring, and because the last thing they want is to be bored, they decide they won't pray. They do this even though they know God told them to pray, even though the Scriptures tell them to pray, even though they know what it does. It's boring, so they don't do it.

Part of the reason is that they haven't disciplined themselves to get information about which they can pray. If you want to know how to pray for someone, do a study of all the prayers of the Bible. Discipline yourself to investigate biblical praying, and then work your way through each one of those prayers, inserting the name of the person you are concerned about. That will keep you going for a bit.

Then make sure you have all the information you can get about the ministries of your own church. When you see a list of small group studies or care groups, copy it and pray for each of them. Get a list of the missionaries your church supports and pray for each one. Get information from the missions office about their needs and concerns. Keep yourself informed from Scripture about the will of God, from people about the circumstances of people, and notice what Paul says: You've got to do it "watchfully," which means "alertly." Keep your eyes wide open to what is going on in the world around you, and pray accordingly. This is the discipline of information.

Second, prayer is a discipline of inspiration. Prayer is only effective as we pray in the Spirit. That means a disciplined life where we keep in step with the Spirit. It means that we know what it means to be living in the fullness of the Spirit. We discipline ourselves so that we are laying aside old ways, we are putting to death old lifestyles, we're concentrating upon all the instructions we've gone through in Colossians. And as we discipline our lives, we begin to discover the inspiration of the Spirit.

Prayer is also perspiration. Notice that Epaphras in 4:12 is described as "wrestling in prayer." The word is "agonizing" in prayer, the same word Paul used in 2:1 to describe his own efforts.

Have you ever agonized in prayer? I have. I've agonized to try to get some time to do it with everything else I have on my schedule. I've agonized to keep concentrating on it when I'm trying to do it. I find my timetable filled with good things, I find my mind filled with other things, and when I eventually find the time and the concentration, the phone rings.

You try and you try and you try, and you look at the problems people have, and you say, "What possible answers are there to these things?" In prayer you take the burden off of yourself and you roll it onto God. That's perspiration!

Prayer is a discipline of information, of inspiration, of perspiration. But it's also a discipline of continuation.

It's not uncommon to see people start off in a big way and fizzle in a hurry. I much prefer to see people start the other way and grow.

In 1857, Jeremiah Lanphier invited the people of New York to meet with him to pray for a revival in Manhattan. Out of one million people, six came. But he continued with it, stuck to it, and one year later *six thousand people met daily at the noon hour in the churches of Manhattan to pray for revival.* Tens of thousands met in the evenings to pray for revival. The word spread to Chicago, and from Chicago to the mission fields of the world. This was known as the Third Great Awakening.

Have you ever thought of being a person who would keep his eyes on the throne, relate what he sees there to the people with whom he rubs shoulders, and pray that God would move among his friends, family, and acquaintances? Have you thought to make a declaration of your priorities in life by disciplining yourself to pray, despite all the other things that clamor for your attention? Might you be one who, through prayer, will keep looking up?

William Wilberforce, the author of *Real Christianity* and a personal friend of William Pitt the younger, could have been Prime Minister of Great Britain. He turned it down because he said he had two objectives: The abolition of slavery, and reformation of national morals.

"Boldly I must confess that I believe the national difficulties we face result from the decline of religion and morality among us," he said. "I must confess equally boldly that my own solid hopes for the well-being of my country depend not so much on her navies and armies, not on the wisdom of her rulers, nor on the spirit of her people, as on the persuasion that she still contains many who love and obey the gospel of Christ. I believe that their prayers may yet prevail."

Would that apply to our nation at this time in history? What do you look to, our navies, armies and air force, our SDI? What are we looking to, our rulers? Are you looking to the president or to congress to pull us out of the mess? Do we look to the wonderful spirit of the people? Do we still quote that old Frenchman who came here a couple of hundred years ago who said that America is great because America is good? Are we pinning our hopes on these things?

Or do we believe that if anything is going to happen in America to turn things around and impact the world, that it will be God's people who know how to pray and who do it?

How Can I Get Involved?

I endorse what Wilberforce said. I believe this is a message for each of us.

Will you join me?

The Declaration of Dependence

Devote yourselves to prayer,
being ... thankful.

When invading Japanese armies forced General Douglas MacArthur to evacuate the Philippines at the outset of World War II, he made a famous declaration: "I shall return."

It wasn't a prayer, but at that stage of the conflict it might well have been. MacArthur was convinced the tide would turn, and he put himself on record as predicting it. He turned out to be right. He did return, and he vindicated his declaration.

Christian prayer is every bit the declaration that MacArthur's statement was. In fact, it's more so. When a person prays, he is making a statement. His prayer is first of all a declaration of dependence. Not a declaration of *independence*, but of dependence. When a man or woman believes in prayer and practices it, that man or woman is declaring his utter dependence upon God.

It stands to reason that any Christian really thinking about it would have to admit that prayerlessness is sheer arrogance. If I don't bother to pray, what I am really saying is, "I can make it alone. I can handle this."

How Can I Get Involved?

What often happens is that people who assume they can make it alone get into desperate straits. And then what do they do? They turn to God—and would you believe, they expect him to be waiting, listening, and ready with an answer yesterday. That's arrogance.

There are people who believe that God was the one who initiated their salvation, that God sent Christ, made him to be sin, and judged him for our sins. They believe with all their hearts that God raised him from the dead and took him to his own right hand, and they believe it is God, by his Spirit, who touched their hearts and opened their minds to the gospel and drew them to himself.

They believe that God did all this, and then for some strange reason they embark on an utterly prayerless life of what they call "Christian discipleship." How arrogant can they be?

They know it was God who initiated their experience; they assume that it is they who perpetuate it. Their total lack of dependence upon him demonstrates it. Conversely, the person of prayer is constantly affirming his or her dependence upon the Lord. Prayerfulness is evidence of faithfulness. Prayer is a declaration of dependence.

It also declares our delight. Notice that in verse 2 Paul includes the word "thankful." He has already talked about being utterly devoted to the risen Christ with particular reference to his majesty. Now he says that when we pray to the risen Christ seated at the Father's right hand, it is good to express our devotion. Whenever we sing praises in the community of believers, or hum while driving along the freeway, we express devotion to the majestic Lord.

Paul is especially interested here in the type of prayer we call "intercession," for he is asking that they pray on his behalf so that the ministry might go forward. But he also recognizes that thanksgiving and praise are an integral part of prayer.

When we turn to prayer and do it thankfully, we are expressing our gratitude to God. Common courtesy insists that we say "Thank you."

When I was a little boy I once came to my mother with a request.

"I want some bread," I said.

248

"What else do you say?" she asked.

"I want some jam, too."

What she wanted to hear, of course, was the word "please." When I eventually got the bread, but not the jam, I said, "Now I want some jam."

"What else do you say?"

"I just said it! I want some jam."

"You say, 'Thank you,' young man."

Common courtesy says that we try to knock into our little kids' heads the phrases "please" and "thank you." Common courtesy requires it.

If that's true in everyday, ordinary human activity, how much more so in reference to God? The believer is a person who, in prayer, is making a constant declaration of delight in God. He has a constant attitude of gratitude, he gives a continual paean of praise. That's what prayer means. It is a declaration of delight.

I conducted a funeral service not long ago. At the beginning of the service I reminded the people why we were there. It's always good to remind ourselves why we are in a certain place doing what we are doing. We were there to remember the one who had died. We were there to speak well of her, to bring encouragement and help to those who had been bereaved. But we were also there to worship.

I took a minute or two to explain the third one; the first two are obvious. Why do you worship at a funeral? You worship at a funeral because it is God who initiates life, and the person who was being buried that day had been alive 75 years, 6 months and 1 day. Seventy-five and one-half years previously God had brought that person into existence through the miracle of birth. For 75 1/2 years, through all kinds of remarkable circumstances, God had perpetuated the life that he initiated.

But then one week in the middle of the night he touched her and called her home to himself. God initiated, God perpetuated, until God terminated. Or as Job put it, "The Lord has given, the Lord has taken away, blessed be the name of the Lord."

You worship at funerals. At funerals you are thankful. At funerals you express gratitude. Why? Because as you are confronted with the person who has died, you are reminded that God and God alone initiates, perpetuates, and terminates life, and for this you give him thanks. If this is true at a funeral, it is absolutely true everywhere else.

Those who know how to pray are those who devote themselves to prayer thankfully, and their prayer itself is a declaration of sheer delight in who God is and what he has done.

Have you learned the common spiritual courtesies of "please" and "thank you"? They are well worth your time—and the issues involved are infinitely more substantial than a spoonful of jam.

Unsung Heroes

*Epaphras, who is one of you and a servant of
Christ Jesus, sends greetings. He is always
wrestling in prayer for you, that you may stand
firm in all the will of God, mature and fully
assured.*

Not all great heroes have famous names. Some do their mighty works quietly, out of the limelight. I read of one such man the other day.

This particular man had only a sixth-grade education. He was a committed Christian, and one day told his church that he wanted to teach a Sunday school class. He was advised none were available, but that he could round up a few strays and begin one with them if he'd like.

Eventually he gathered a class of thirteen rowdy boys, nine from broken homes. He loved those kids. He took them hiking. He played marbles with them. He cared, and his kids knew it.

Today, eleven of those thirteen boys are in full-time vocational Christian work. Howard Hendricks, whom I mentioned earlier, was one of those boys. Hendricks tells this man's story in his book *Teaching to Change Lives*.

The Colossians had a man like that in their corner. Paul names Epaphras as the one responsible for planting the church in Colossae, and lauds him for his continuing concern for the church there: "Epaphras, who is one of you and a servant of Christ

Jesus, sends greetings. He is always wrestling in prayer for you, that you may stand firm in all the will of God, mature and fully assured."

Epaphras was a man of prayer, and his particular prayer for the people in Colossae was that those who had started well might stand firm. He prayed that those who had moved into newness of life might become fully assured of it. He thoroughly believed that prayer helps growing believers to mature.

Is there any need for that kind of praying today? There surely is.

Can you think of one person who, at one time in his life, was really interested in the things of Christ, but who now no longer takes his stand in him?

Can you think of one person who began to show signs of spiritual life, but who never matured?

Can you think of people who began to learn the things of Christ, but then saw the ground taken out from under them and are no longer assured of the truth of the gospel? Can you think of anyone? I assure you that I can. And I'm sure you can, too.

Let's bring it a little closer to home. Can you think of anyone who used to run well with the Lord Jesus in your own church? Can you think of anybody who used to stand firm in Christ? Can you think of anybody who used to speak out for the Lord Jesus and bear a consistent testimony, but today is nowhere to be found? Can you think of anyone who fell by the wayside?

The hard question is this: Do we pray for these people? Do we recognize that the only way they will be turned to God is if God, by his power, reaches out to them from heaven and touches them in response to the believing prayer of God's people?

Prayer moves God to open doors, helps mold people together, makes witnesses adequate, and helps mature growing believers.

Are you engaging in that kind of prayer? Are you responding positively to the apostle's challenge? What a tremendous need there is for people who will take this seriously.

John Wesley put it this way: "Give me 100 preachers who fear nothing but sin and desire nothing but God, and I care not a straw whether they be clergy or laity. Such alone will shake the gates of hell and set up the Kingdom of Heaven on earth. God does nothing but in answer to prayer."

I listen to a man like John Wesley, because he was a man in touch with heaven. He was a man who could translate the power of heaven into the situation on earth.

Wesley was credited, along with his little group of preachers, with saving Britain from something as drastic and bloody and horrible as the French Revolution. He was instrumental in establishing hundreds of churches and winning thousands of people to Christ at a time when Britain was in dire and desperate straits.

He was a man who knew God.

So when a man like John Wesley says a thing like that, I think the church in all generations should listen hard and ask itself, "Are we a praying church that is in touch with the sheer power of God?"

That's a question for all of us to answer. The sooner we answer it positively, the closer we are to recruiting the kind of force that Wesley envisioned.

Wesley's brother, Charles, once wrote a hymn dealing with some of these very issues. I think it would be appropriate to end the chapter on his note:

Ye servants of God, your Master proclaim,
And publish abroad His wonderful name;
The name, all victorious, of Jesus extol:
His kingdom is glorious, He rules over all.

God ruleth on high, almighty to save,
And still He is nigh, His presence we have;
The great congregation His triumph shall sing,
Ascribing salvation to Jesus, our King.

"Salvation to God, who sits on the throne!"
Let all cry aloud, and honor the Son;
The praises of Jesus the angels proclaim,
Fall down on their faces and worship the Lamb.

Then let us adore, and give Him His right—
All glory and pow'r, all wisdom and might,
All honor and blessing, with angels above,
And thanks never ceasing, and infinite love.

Open Doors

And pray for us, too, that God may open a door for our message, so that we may proclaim the mystery of Christ, for which I am in chains.

pen doors are wonderful things. Without them, you could crash all day into the side of your refrigerator and never once get inside.

Open doors allow you to get to people. Closed doors keep you out. The apostle Paul apparently thought a lot about this.

More than once he talked about God opening doors of opportunity. After Paul and Barnabas had gone on their missionary journey, they returned to their sending church in Antioch and reported all that had happened. Among other things, they said that God had opened the door of faith to the Gentiles.

God has to open those doors if anything is to happen. Unless God intervenes, nothing of eternal consequence will be accomplished. There's a danger that as we become better equipped technologically, as we get our methodology oiled and honed and improved, we'll think we can get the job done by ourselves. How foolish that is!

When you deal with souls, you are dabbling in eternal issues. Ministry is a battle. Because it's a battle and because the opposition is formidable, we need resources greater than our own technology and methodology and enthusiasm and money. We need God to open doors.

Currently there are more than thirty countries which restrict missionary activity. Those thirty-plus countries account for two-fifths of the world's population. Humanly speaking, two-fifths of the world is nearly out of reach. What shall we do? Do we shrug our shoulders, or do we take to heart Paul's instruction to pray that God might open doors?

Andrew Murray put it this way: "There is a world with its needs, entirely dependent upon and waiting to be helped by intercession. There is a God in heaven with his all-sufficient supply for all those needs, waiting to be asked. There is a church with its wondrous calling and its sure promises, waiting to be roused to a sense of its wondrous responsibility and power. There is a world with its perishing millions, with intercession its only hope."

In the second week of July, 1986, the five billionth baby was born into the world. There are more people alive on earth at the present time than ever before. The population of the world has been increasing each week by about the size of Milwaukee.

It took until 1830 to produce the first billion. It took one hundred years to produce the second billion. From 1930 to 1986 we produced three billion more. There will be six billion plus by the turn of the century. I haven't bothered calculating after that.

What worries me is that of the five billion people on the face of God's earth, more than half are to all intents and purposes unreached with the gospel of Christ. At least one billion are eminently reachable, but aren't being touched.

So what are we doing about it? Are we the kind of people who declare our utter devotion to the majesty of Christ through intercessory prayer? Or have we gotten so wrapped up in ourselves that we have lost sight of the God of the throne and of his world of intense need?

Henry Martyn had a brilliant career as a mathematician at Cambridge University. While there he became involved in the church where Charles Simeon was minister. Soon he decided to go into the ministry and became Simeon's assistant.

After serving there a short time, he felt constrained to become the first volunteer to a new missionary society going out to India. The day he arrived at his new home he wrote in his journal, "Now let me burn out for God."

If Henry Martyn came back today, he'd look at all the books on "burnout" and say, "Great! All these people want to burn out for God!" But then he would read the books and discover that they were trying to ensure that, whatever else would happen, people *wouldn't* burn out.

Now, I understand what these books are saying. I realize that people can get tired and exhausted. I understand and sympathize with it. But I also have a deep concern that many segments of the church lack any devotion to the ministry of Christ. People no longer say, "Let's go get it, let's do it, and if we burn out while doing it, hallelujah anyway!"

Henry Martyn, incidentally, translated the New Testament into Hindustani. When he finished that he translated it into Arabic. When he finished that he translated it into Persian—and he was a mathematician, not a linguist. When he completed that, he died. He was thirty-one years old.

Paul was a man like that. He didn't sit in his prison cell saying, "Well, here I am stuck in prison. I guess I'll let those other guys do it now." No, he said, "Here I am, stuck in prison. Pray that God will open some doors—perhaps, first of all, that he'll open the cell doors here so I can get out. Next, pray for open doors that will allow us to get to places we haven't been."

Paul had Kingdom on his mind. He was committed to seeing his Lord's prayer fulfilled: "Our Father, who art in heaven, hallowed be thy name. Thy kingdom come, thy will be done on earth as it is in heaven."

Is that a prayer you've said recently? Have you asked yourself, "What exactly am I doing to bring about the establishment of the kingdom on earth so that the will of God might be done on earth as it is in heaven"?

I got a letter one day from a Thomas Samuel, a missionary working among the unreached tribal villages of India. Christians had been praying that God would intervene in the utter pagan ignorance of these tribes. The area was suffering through a terrible drought, and believers began praying that God would send rain. He did.

The pagans who heard these prayers were convinced that God had heard and answered. They had lived through other droughts and knew the horrors they could bring. Now they began to turn to the Lord.

God was opening doors.

I received a letter from Argentina describing an evangelist who often holds a series of meetings in a great soccer stadium where anywhere from fifty to eighty thousand people give their lives to Christ each week. That's fifty to eighty thousand Argentines *per week* who respond to the gospel. God is doing something utterly inexplicable in human terms.

God is opening doors.

Why does this happen? It happens because people take seriously the instruction of Scripture to pray that God will open doors. God does this because he is a God with a plan. But as Norwegian theologian Professor Hallesby says, "He governs with a degree of elasticity."

God has a plan and will bring it about, but there is such elasticity in it that it can be accomplished in all kinds of ways. God works in response to the prevailing prayer of his people. He will change lives. He will change circumstances. He will intervene in government. He will intervene in nature.

God opens doors.

The encouraging thing about this is that he usually opens them wide enough so that several people together can get through. Evangelism is a team effort. Notice what Paul said: "And pray for *us*, too, that God may open a door."

Who is he referring to? The rest of the chapter lists all the people who worked with him, people with wonderful names like Tychicus and Aristarchus and Barnabas, Epaphras, Demas, Nympha, and Archippus. Wouldn't you love to be with a group like that? You'd find wonderful nicknames for them all, I'm sure. Paul called them fellow-soldiers, fellow-servants, fellow-sufferers. They were with Paul in ministry.

God usually does not work through a single individual. Normally he works through people who are knit together in a team. Nobody demonstrated that better than Paul.

It's obvious from his letters that people are with him, even as he is in prison. He is "in chains" even as he writes this letter, but his friends are with him even there. They are part of the team. Paul says it is imperative that you pray for the team.

Why? For one simple yet profound reason. If the devil wants to stop evangelism, all he has to do is to get Christians fighting with each other. It's so easy for him. If he wants to deflect people from what they're supposed to be doing, all he has to do is to get them squabbling. If he wants to make the work of Christ grind to a halt, he'll get people to major on minors.

When the apostle says, "Pray for us," he means it. He had a job to do, and he couldn't afford to get waylaid because people failed to pray for his team. I'm convinced Paul's instruction is a message for the church throughout the ages.

Are you praying that God would open doors of opportunity for Christians to declare the gospel? Are you taking advantage of the doors God gives you?

What would you think of someone who found a cure for cancer but didn't share it? What would you think if he defended his silence by saying, "Well, it's very personal. I couldn't possibly tell you. Besides, I don't want to ram my cure down anyone's throat"?

You wouldn't be terribly impressed.

How often have you met people who profess to belong to Christ who say the same sorts of things about their faith?

We need to decide if what we have discovered in Christ is of greater significance than a cure for cancer. If it is, we had better determine to devote ourselves to him and to tell others what we know of him.

You can start by asking God to open a door of opportunity.

Don't be surprised if he asks you to walk through it!

On the Inside Looking Out

*Pray that I may proclaim [the gospel] clearly, as
I should. Be wise in the way you act toward
outsiders; make the most of every opportunity. Let
your conversation be always full of grace,
seasoned with salt, so that you may know how to
answer everyone.*

Who says God doesn't play football?

"God," Mike shouted, "if you'll let my kid score a
touchdown, I'll be in church next Sunday!"

It was quite a statement. Mike hadn't gone to church in
years, and he had no intention of going now. But desperation
changes the rules. His son's football team had gone scoreless after
six games, and he figured the only hope left was prayer.

On the very next play Mike's son was given the ball, a hole
opened up in the line, and he raced 60 yards to score a touchdown.
The crowd went wild, and Mike's buddies reminded him of his
oath: "So, Saint Mike, you'll be in church next Sunday? Right?"

"I'll be there," Mike promised. He had no trouble choosing
a church, because sitting next to him was a Christian friend whose
son also played on the team.

Mike came to church, heard the gospel, and came to Christ.
Two weeks later his son became a Christian.[1]

Why did it happen? According to Joe Aldrich, who tells
this story, it happened because a Christian dad made a deliberate

decision to make friends with non-Christians. When God intervened in Mike's life, a concerned Christian was there. Mike's conversion was no accident.

Paul's strategy was similar. The apostle not only asked that his Colossian friends pray that he and his companions might be effective in their ministry, but he reminds the Colossians that they, too, have a ministry. While in verse 4 he says, "Pray that I may proclaim the gospel clearly, as I should," in verse 5 he immediately applies it to them and says, "Be wise in the way you act toward outsiders."

He reminds them that the work of ministry, the work of disseminating the Christian gospel, is not the work of a favored elite. It is not the work of a relatively small group of professionals. It is the work of all believers.

"I believed, therefore I have spoken," says the Old Testament as quoted by Paul in 2 Corinthians 4:13. "Let the redeemed of the Lord say this," says Psalm 107:2. And Romans 10 reminds us that if we confess with our mouths as well as believe in our hearts, we shall be saved. Open articulation of the faith is part and parcel of every Christian's spiritual experience.

Many people admit they feel desperately inadequate to the task. If you feel like this, join the club. Lots of us feel the same way. Don't worry about feeling inadequate; feel worried if you *don't* feel inadequate. Anybody who glibly and superficially storms into the business of communicating the Christian gospel has not understood the sheer immensity of what he is doing.

Many years ago Jill was working with a group of young people, trying to encourage them and train them to go out and share their faith. They were going to visit the coffee houses and dance halls, and she asked me to have a final word with them. I agreed.

I told these young people that they must not forget that as soon as they began to talk to people about Jesus Christ, they were dabbling with eternal souls. They would be messing with eternal issues, and they were going to engage the spiritual forces of darkness. Their faces dropped quite dramatically as I explained all this.

My wife had a little talk with me afterwards.

"I took about four weeks pumping up these kids, and it takes you about five minutes to stick a pin in them," she said.

"All I did was to remind them that if they go out seeking to minister to people on any other basis than in the anointing of the Holy Spirit, anticipating his intervention through the power of God, they are going to fail," I replied.

She agreed with my theology, but not with my methods.

For anyone to speak adequately the message of Christ, to know what to say, to know how to say it, to know whom to say it to, to say it in such a way that it will be acceptable and understandable and will elicit a favorable response, demands more intelligence than the sum of every congregation in the world. It requires that God, by his Spirit, speak his Word through people's lips, under the anointing of the Spirit and with his own brand of miracles. That is what Paul is saying here.

He put it in very practical terms. He says, "Be wise in the way you act toward outsiders." In other words, if you don't build good relationships, why should anyone listen to you? "Make the most of every opportunity." If the chance to communicate the truth comes your way, don't miss it. "Let your conversation always be full of grace." Don't expect people to listen to your report of Christ if at other times your mouth is as dirty and filthy as the rest of them. Make sure that what you say is "seasoned with salt," that it's appetizing, that it's interesting, that it has a tang to it, that it captures their imagination and holds their attention. And ask God to show you "how to answer everyone."

That doesn't mean you must have all the answers. It does mean that you're ready to hear their questions and then respond as best you're able.

You say, "Stuart, this makes me feel so inadequate!"

I hope it does. Do you know why? If you feel adequate in your abilities, you'll go out bumping around in your own power and make an absolute mess of things. No, make sure you are inadequate, then get on your knees and pray for yourself and for others. Say, "God, intervene in my life and in their lives so that we might become adequate witnesses of Jesus Christ."

God answers those kinds of prayers. Believe me, he will. If he answers prayers that knock open holes in an opposing team's line so that a scoreless, 0-6 football team can notch its first touchdown, he'll answer a prayer that asks him to make you an effective witness for Jesus Christ.

But be prepared for surprises. You never know how he might answer.

Right, Mike?

1. Joseph C. Aldrich, *Gentle Persuasion: Creative Ways to Introduce Your Friends to Christ*, (Portland, Ore.: Multnomah Press, 1988), pp. 23,24.

Spreading Like Wildfire

All over the world this gospel is producing fruit and growing, just as it has been doing among you since the day you heard it and understood God's grace in all its truth. You learned it from Epaphras, our dear fellow servant, who is a faithful minister of Christ on our behalf . . .

Have you ever wondered how all the New Testament churches got started? Most were located in utterly pagan cities whose inhabitants had no knowledge of Christ at all. How do you think those churches got started?

You say, "Well, probably what happened was that one day everyone was busy in the marketplace and suddenly the clouds parted and a bright light shone and a voice thundered, 'Let me introduce you to my Son, Jesus.'"

No, it didn't work that way so far as we know. God has an unbelievably simple method, and here it is: People who know God explain what they know to others who don't know. They have a message, and they deliver it.

Paul describes this message as "God's grace in all its truth." It is called "the gospel which is fruitful and growing all over the world," "the word of truth that has come to you." Paul says his message has come from God to Colossae, a message of God's grace (an undeserved gift) and truth (as against the city's superstition). The message came to people where they were.

How does God move into people's lives today? The message of his grace gets out to people through studies in office blocks, at downtown lunch hour meetings in hotels, on television programs, in dramatic presentations. God uses all these methods so that his message of grace and truth might come to people where they are.

This is why some people will sit down and share with their friends what they've discovered, so that the message of God's grace might come to people where they are. That's the business we're in. That is why we exist as people alive in Christ in cities and towns across the globe.

Notice that no one gets the message without a messenger. Paul says he delivered the message of God's grace to the Colossians, but so far as we know he never even visited the city. Do you know how he pulled it off?

When he was in Ephesus, he discovered that a Greek teacher by the name of Tyrannus had a school. Tyrannus didn't have classes in the middle of the day because it was too hot. Everybody took a siesta (or the Greek equivalent) in the afternoon, so Paul went to Tyrannus and said, "Could I borrow your school-room in the heat of the day?"

"What for?" Tyrannus asked.

"I'd like to teach a class," Paul replied.

"Nobody'll come in the heat of the day!"

"Don't you worry about that. Can I have it?"

"Sure, for all the good it'll do you."

So Paul got his classroom. I've been to Ephesus a number of times, and each time I go they've unearthed something else. The last time I was there, they announced they had discovered the site of the school of Tyrannus. Paul saw this school when it was fresh and nice, and told the believers in Ephesus, "I'm going to teach theology in the middle of the day, in the heat of the day, when everybody else is in the sack. You guys get yourselves out of the sack and get yourselves here. I'm going to teach you."

People came, and every day for two solid years Paul taught in the school of Tyrannus. Acts 19 tells us the most remarkable thing about these classes. Their influence wasn't restricted to Ephesus: "All that dwelt in Asia heard the word of the Lord."

Have you ever read that? How on earth could that be?

Let me remind you quickly that the Asia it talks about isn't the Asia of today. It was the Roman province of Asia, where Colossae, Hierapolis, Laodicea, Phrygia, Troas, and many other cities were to be found.

Because Paul taught for two years in Ephesus, every single one of these cities heard the word of the Lord—even though Paul never visited any of them. How did it work?

Sitting in class was a little fellow named Epaphras. You wouldn't notice him, just an ordinary little guy. Not an apostle or anything like that. He hadn't been to seminary, hadn't gone to Bible school, didn't have "Reverend" in front of his name. He was just an ordinary little guy, sitting in the back row taking notes, studying his Bible. He didn't know beforehand that he could study it. He hadn't the faintest idea he could do theology. If you had suggested it to him, he might have had a pink fit.

But he sat down in class, taking it all in. Then one day Paul said, "Okay, folks, now this is what I want you to do. Everything you've learned, go tell somebody else."

Epaphras put up his hand and said, "Where should I start?"

"Well, where do you live?" Paul asked.

"Colossae," Epaphras replied.

"Start there," Paul said, so little Epaphras took his three ring binder and his New International Version Study Bible and off he went to Colossae. He began with people he knew and started to share what he knew—that's from the human level. But from the divine point of view, the gospel of the grace of God in all its truth was coming to Colossae.

How on earth are we going to reach our own communities? I sit and think about this all the time. What should we do in Milwaukee, for instance?

I received a letter one day that reminded me of something very special. Many years ago, probably almost 70 years ago now, a young boy in England went to camp. He went from a family that was not too enthusiastic about his going. It was a Christian camp, and the family wasn't Christian. While he was there this young boy came to Christ. His name was Ian Thomas.

Ian went off to medical school. He'd only been there a few weeks when he was invited to speak at a Christian conference where the scheduled speaker had taken ill. The dean of the medical college gave him permission to leave school, provided he returned to school immediately after he was done with the meetings. He made that promise and left.

He still hasn't gone back. He's in his middle 70s now, and he's never stopped preaching.

One day Ian was driving along the autobahn in Germany. He saw a boy hitchhiking, but because his car was already overloaded, he drove on past. Suddenly he thought, *I've got to pick up that kid*, so he stopped his car right on the autobahn, put it in reverse, and scurried back.

The kid's name was Peter Wiegand, a long, lanky 17-year-old from Hamburg. Pete got to sit on the gear shift because the car was so overloaded that the shifter kept slipping out of gear.

Ian shared his sandwich and his experience of Christ with Pete. The boy came back to England with him to mingle in a little Bible school there, and soon he came to faith in Christ.

Pete sat in the school of Tyrannus for a couple of years, then left for Austria. He started a similar school there called Schlossklaus. One of the first people he met when he got to Austria was Ernst Thaler. Pete led Ernst to Christ, Ernst went home and told his brother Walter what had happened, and Walter came to faith in Christ, too.

One day Walter was driving on the autobahn when he noticed a kid thumbing a ride. He recalled something of his own spiritual heritage, so he stopped his car and picked up the boy. He discovered the lad was a Japanese named Tana. Tana came to the school of Tyrannus, hung around for a bit, and eventually came to faith in Jesus.

Why do I tell you all this? Because through the work of the Torchbearers, an exciting ministry began a few years ago in Japan where less than half of one percent of the population believes in Jesus. That ministry began because of Tana, and Tana because of Walter, and Walter because of Ernst, and Ernst because of Peter, and Peter because of Ian, and Ian because of an unknown man way, way back. That's how it works.

When people like Paul and Epaphras go wherever God sends them, taking the trouble to know what they believe and share what they believe and to demonstrate the reality of it in their lives, God works and brings people to faith in Christ.

The method is quite simple. People simply tell what they know, and as a result others hear and understand and learn and believe and do and tell. As a result somebody else hears and understands and believes, and the whole thing repeats itself.

Here is a little mathematical problem for you. Work it out with me. One hundred people each lead one person to Christ in one year. How many have you got at the end of a year? That's right, 200.

The same thing happens the next year. Now how many have you got? That's right, 400. After three years we're up to 800. The next year it goes to 1,600, then 3,200, then 6,400, 12,800, 25,600, 51,200, 102,400. One hundred people have become 100,000, allowing for 2,400 backsliders in ten years.

Do you get the picture? And yet people scratch their heads and say, "How on earth are we going to do it?"

The answer is basic and obvious, right under our very noses. When you produce people who know what they believe and why they believe it, people who get out there and live it and share it, God works. It's that simple.

Are you interested in growing spiritually? This is a good place to start. Do this, and not only will you grow in your spiritual life, but you'll begin to discover—as Paul said at Colossae—that the gospel is growing and bearing fruit all over the world.

Your little corner of the world, too.

Working Out

1. Paul uses an interesting pair of words in Colossians 4:2 to encourage his friends to pray. The NIV says "*Devote* yourselves to prayer, being *watchful* . . ." The word translated "devoted" means "to busy oneself with," "be busily engaged in." It carries the idea of intense activity, of vigorous action. The word translated "watchful" means to "be wide awake about it." The interesting thing is the connection between the apostle's call for vigorous prayer and his caution that it can make you sleepy.

This connection occurs in other parts of Scripture, too. Matthew 26:36-46 tells the story of Jesus' agonizing time of prayer in the garden of Gethsemane. He takes along Peter and James and John and says to them, "My soul is overwhelmed with sorrow to the point of death. Stay here and *keep watch* [the same word as in Colossians 4:2] with me." What happens? All three disciples fall asleep. When Jesus finds them sleeping, he says to Peter, "Could you men not *keep watch* with me one hour? *Watch* and *pray* so that you will not fall into temptation. The spirit is willing, but the body is weak." Twice more he leaves the trio to pray, and each time he returns to find them sleeping.

In 1 Thessalonians 5:5-6, Paul exhorts the church to remain vigilant in their faith. He talks about unbelievers who are unready for the Lord's coming, and says they will be taken by surprise by it. Then he writes, "Let us not be like others, who are asleep, but let us *be alert* [the same word translated "keep watch"] and self-controlled."

A. Do you find that you become sleepy when you try to pray? What clues can you find in the words of Jesus and of Paul that might help you to stay awake? Do they see this as an easy thing to do, or something requiring great effort? Why do they say we should expend such effort?

2. Paul mentions five important things about effective evangelism in Colossians 4:5-6. On a separate sheet of paper, list each of the five things and in your own words describe how you would accomplish them. After you have your list finished, turn to Acts 17:16-34; 23:1-11; 26:1-29. In each case, note to whom Paul was speaking and how he adapted his message to each group. What can we learn from his methods?

Second Wind

1. Ecclesiastes 4:9-12
   Does anyone in your life come immediately to mind when you read these verses? If so, let him know!

2. 1 Thessalonians 3:6-10
   What one thing about the Thessalonians encouraged Paul more than anything else?

3. 1 Samuel 12:23-24
   How would the prophet Samuel have regarded himself had he neglected to pray for his people?

4. 2 Corinthians 5:11-21
   Is Paul just talking about himself and his friends in this passage, or does it refer to us? How do we know?

5. Hebrews 13:1-3, 18
   What practical suggestions does this passage give for carrying out the command of verse 1?

V
Christian Warnings

Staying on Track

What Are Wolves Doing Here?

*I tell you this so that no one may deceive you
by fine-sounding arguments.*
Colossians 2:4

*See to it that no one takes you captive through hollow and deceptive
philosophy, which depends on human tradition and the basic
principles of this world rather than on Christ.*
Colossians 2:8

*Therefore do not let anyone judge you by what you eat or drink, or
with regard to a religious festival, a New Moon celebration or a
Sabbath day. These are a shadow of the things that were to come;
the reality, however, is found in Christ.*

*Do not let anyone who delights in false humility and the worship
of angels disqualify you for the prize. Such a person goes into great
detail about what he has seen, and his unspiritual mind puffs him
up with idle notions. He has lost connection with the Head, from
whom the whole body, supported and held together by its ligaments
and sinews, grows as God causes it to grow.*

*Since you died with Christ to the basic principles of this world,
why, as though you still belonged to it, do you submit to its rules:
"Do not handle! Do not taste! Do not touch!"? These are all destined
to perish with use, because they are based on human commands
and teachings. Such regulations indeed have an appearance of
wisdom, with their self-imposed worship, their false humility and
their harsh treatment of the body, but they lack any value in
restraining sensual indulgence.*
Colossians 2:16-23

Beware!
That's the Shallow End
He's Pushing You In!

One of the most valuable things you can take on a trip south of the border is a bit of advice: Don't drink the water.

One of the best items to pack for a canoeing expedition down a dangerous river is a caution: Don't stand up in the canoe.

And one of the kindest presents you can give a young man searching for love is surely this: Don't marry any girl who smokes the wrong end of a lit cigar.

Warnings. They're indispensable to life. If heeded, they can save you untold heartache and misery.

That's why Paul's letter to the Colossians would be incomplete without some sober cautions against enemies who would try to lure believers away from Christ. Warnings are necessary and good. Sometimes they can save your life.

Have you ever watched a weightlifting competition? You marvel as contestant after enormous contestant strains to manhandle several hundred pounds of dead weight—biceps bulging, chests heaving, necks swelling, sweat pouring off gargantuan physiques. You wonder how long it took them to gain such fearsome strength, what sacrifices they made to get it, what their grocery bill looks like. But more than anything, you notice the faces.

Grim faces. Determined faces. Faces that look like they could eat iron as well as pump it.

Some of these faces look like they'd do anything for an extra advantage. And some of them do. One of the most common ways of gaining advantage is through drugs—an illicit advantage, surely, but an advantage nonetheless. "If it works, why not?" goes the reasoning.

That's why a group of substances called "anabolic steroids," or simply "steroids," exploded in popularity in the recent past. Though banned from today's contests, they'd been used for years by a few pioneers to increase muscle strength and bulk. Only recently did their use become widespread.

It's not hard to imagine how an athlete, spurred on by overzealous advisors, would react to something that promised significant advantage.

"Come on, Charlie, just try it. Look what it's done for Pete!"

"I don't know, Bill. I've won my weight division the last three years without that stuff. Why start now?"

"Get with it, man! Just think how much stronger it'll make you. Think of the advantage!"

"I'm still not sure. Are there any side effects?"

"Look, if you don't want my help, I'll find someone who does. Do you really think your opponents are going to let something like this pass by? Your old methods were OK, but this stuff will set you up for life. Look—do you want my help or not?"

"OK, OK. I suppose it couldn't hurt."

It's true that steroids give an advantage.

It's also true, the medical world has discovered, that they gain that advantage by wrecking any body that consumes them. That's the trade: Consume them, they consume you. And not just for a few years of competition, but for life.

Occasionally you'll see a sad report of an aging, steroid-using former weightlifter whose body lies in shambles. He'd gotten off-track. He'd listened to advice about a quick and better way to championship belts. He'd allowed a smooth-talking salesman to sell him bottled muscles. He'd used those bottles.

And now he was dying.

The apostle Paul warned the church in Colossae about people who would try to sell them bottles of doctrinal death. He warned them about deceivers who would come into their midst in order to turn them away from the Christ they had learned and loved. He wanted to expose these deceivers before they had a chance to sell their murderous potion.

That's what he says in verse 4: "I tell you all this so that no one may deceive you by fine-sounding arguments."

There are a lot of fine-sounding arguments around. We've learned more about speech communication in this generation than in any one previously. We've thoroughly studied the subject. We know all about public relations, about hidden aspirations. The result has been a proliferation of extremely skilled communication.

That goes for spiritual matters, too. People really know how to put an appeal letter together. They know how to design a radio program, how to lay out books, how to produce television. Among these messages there are many—to use Paul's term—"fine-sounding arguments."

The problem with these fine-sounding arguments is that they'll divert you from Christ. It happened in Colossae, and it happens here. Not infrequently you'll find earnest people who have been beguiled by philosophy or by psychology or by futurology or by astrology. They've been seduced by all kinds of things, wholly caught up in them, and they fail to do one simple, basic thing: They fail to test all their learning against what they have been taught in Christ.

When you do that, you're a sitting duck for all the fine-sounding arguments that come your way. Dick Lucas, writing in his commentary on Colossians, says, "Nothing is so dangerous as feeble reasoning allied with fast talking."

I think that's a significant statement. It's not hard these days to find a lot of feeble reasoning allied to a lot of fast talking. Those Christians who don't take the trouble to make sure they're rooted and grounded in Christ are asking to be swept away into all kinds of deadly nonsense.

What Are Wolves Doing Here?

Paul says, "Recognize that these deceivers will come. Recognize they'll promise you all sorts of things. They'll say you're missing out on the real thing. They'll try to sell you bottles of death. Realize that they're coming and turn away from them. Christ is all you need!"

Are there any salesmen at your door? Are you playing with any of those bottles? Get rid of them!

The only real guarantee any of their products offer is a coffin with your name on it.

Beware!
That Man's a Hijacker!

See to it that no one takes you captive through
hollow and deceptive philosophy, which depends
on human tradition and the basic principles of
this world rather than on Christ.

The passengers were flying along at 35,000 feet, minding their own business, doing all the things that passengers do once they are well into their journey. Suddenly they were interrupted by the sound of the intercom being switched on.

"This is your captain speaking," a voice said. "I have some good news for you, and I have some bad news for you. First the bad news: I regret to inform you that we are lost. And now for the good news: We are making excellent time."

The apostle Paul says to these believers in Colossae, "You've got to understand, folks, that having begun your spiritual odyssey, you need to continue. But remember that it's possible to be enthusiastically pursuing whatever lifestyle you choose and be making great time, yet overlook the fact that you are lost. You don't know where you are."

Notice the word of warning he gives to the Colossians in verse 8: "See to it that no one takes you captive through hollow and deceptive philosophy, which depends on human tradition and the basic principles of this world rather than on Christ."

The words translated "See to it" have a much stronger force in Greek than in English. The original means "beware," "look out," "keep your eyes peeled," "keep your wits about you." Why? Because it's possible for us, having begun in our spiritual journey, to be shanghaied by teachers of hollow and deceptive philosophy. The word translated "take you captive" is used to describe a plunder. It's used of someone who moves into a shaky situation, takes over a person's life, plunders his property, and steals away the people themselves. "Kidnap" would be the word today, or "hijack." Beware of spiritual hijackers.

Another flight was taking off from New York, bound for Miami. Suddenly a man in First Class jumped up, grabbed a flight attendant, seized her hair, twisted it into a knot, held a gun to her head, and said, "Take me to the captain."

The frightened woman took him to the captain. The man maintained his grip on the girl but pointed the gun at the captain.

"Take me to Miami," the gunman said.

"But this *is* the Miami flight," the captain protested.

"Take me to Miami," the hijacker repeated.

"We're *going* to Miami," the captain pleaded.

"That's what they said the last two days," the man said, "but both times I ended up in Havana, Cuba."

That's what happens with hijackers. You start off the way you want to go, and finish up where you don't want to be. Somewhere along the way somebody diverts your life.

Beware of spiritual hijackers! That's Paul's word of warning.

How can you be on the alert? One of the best ways is to learn to recognize their methods.

Some will take you captive through deceptive philosophy. The word "philosophy" here does not necessarily mean the kind you learn in college. Paul's not taking a swipe at the study of philosophy.

Philosophia, the Greek term from which we get our English word, simply means "the love of knowledge." Paul is talking about people who just love knowledge, who love teaching, who love learning for what it is in itself. Much of this learning and knowledge and teaching is "empty and deceptive." Paul warns against spiritual hijackers who love to teach you all kinds of things for the sheer joy of teaching so that you would learn for the sheer joy of learning, without ever realizing that the content of this teaching has zero spiritual or eternal value. It is empty and deceptive.

These teachers also will come with traditions that are purely man-made, Paul says. The word "tradition" means "to hand down."

Now, many traditions can be terrifically helpful. Why reinvent the wheel? If someone has invented the wheel, have him hand down wheels to you, and use what he has discovered.

On the other hand, some things handed down to us have long since lost their significance. Once they were helpful; today they're a nuisance.

It's possible, for example, to have a tradition called "Memorial Day" in which people set aside one day a year to remember those who gave their lives in the nation's great wars. It's equally possible, however, for Memorial Day to become a golf outing. The tradition continues, but the significance behind it is utterly and totally lost.

Tradition is not fundamentally wrong, but it can develop into something that is. It's wrong when it merely hands down a shell devoid of substance. It's wrong when it perpetuates a ritual devoid of reality. It's wrong when it invites us to go through the motions with an emptiness of spirit.

Paul says, "Watch people who promote tradition like that, because they'll come into a Christian community and enthusiastically and skillfully promote ideas which are utterly empty and totally useless and which lead ultimately to disaster. They will insist on traditions that have lost all significance and will advocate worldly and destructive thinking."

That's the idea behind verse 8. Paul says these teachers will push a deceptive philosophy which depends on human tradition and the basic principles of this world. When he mentions "this world," he's not against hills and trees and water and birds; he's not opposed to the world of which we're a part. He's talking about a secular system that has no time for God.

People eagerly latch onto the elementary concepts of such a godless system and tie them into traditions. They give them a dash of new teaching and end up with something fascinating and beguiling . . . and utterly empty and deceptive. In the end it will hijack your faith. Why? Because there is one thing wrong with it. They are concentrating on these things—and I quote—"rather than on Christ."

What happens is this. When people come in and begin to hijack your faith by teaching useless traditions and getting you thinking in the wrong way, they will divert your attention from what is right and good and true. They will pervert the gospel by putting in its place those things which rightly belong to Christ. As a result, they subvert the authority of Christ.

Rather than base all spiritual reality and life itself on Christ, where it belongs, they will build all kinds of high-falutin', high-sounding, highly intriguing, wonderfully attractive structures which are at the core empty and destructive. Before you know it, Christ is no longer the believer's authority.

Sounds a bit grim, doesn't it? Paul evidently found it necessary to warn the Colossians about it.

The warning is no less needed today. I suggest we need to take a good, long, hard look at our society and its impact on our churches and our lives.

Would you check to see if somebody has hijacked your faith? Would you check to see if you are continuing as you began? Would you ask yourself, "Am I heeding the warnings of Scripture that remind me how easy it is to get off track, and would I say I am a person who is constantly aware and alert to the manifold spiritual dangers that come my way? Or could it be that I have become so lax and casual and careless and unthinking and unfeeling that I've gotten myself hijacked and have even fallen in love with the hijacker?"

Don't laugh at that last line. It's the sort of thing that really happens when people are hijacked.

It needn't happen to you. When hijackers turn up to steal away your faith, recognize them, resist them, and stand fast in the truth you have learned in Christ. It's the only safe thing to do.

Beware!
That's a Straitjacket
You're Trying On!

*... do not let anyone judge you by what you eat
or drink, or with regard to a religious festival, a
New Moon celebration or a Sabbath day. These
are a shadow of the things that were to come; the
reality, however, is found in Christ.*

I t happened in Münster, Germany, in 1534. A group of sincere but muddle-headed zealots decided Martin Luther's protestant revolution of 1517 hadn't gone far enough. They wanted to live somewhere where "righteousness" truly reigned, and they set out to build such a place.

They moved to Münster and soon were running things, making themselves the unchallenged rulers of a population of 15,000. Before long they had come up with rules for "holy living." All kinds of rules.

Citizens were required to give up their possessions. House doors could not be closed, even at night (although a kind of screen was permitted for keeping out pigs and chickens). Artisans were to work without pay. Quarreling brought the death penalty. All women under a certain age had to marry. Polygamy was enforced.

These rules and many, many more were designed, the town's rulers said, to promote godliness.

What do you suppose was the outcome of all this "enforced righteousness"? Do you think it led to holy living?

You get a clue when you consider that the leader of this madness, John Bockelson, once ran naked through the streets and fell into a trance, awakening several days later to announce a series of "revelations"—which the people accepted!

A few months later Bockelson and a good number of the people of Münster lay dead at the hands of opposing armies who had besieged and sacked the town. So ended one of the sadder episodes of European history.

Bockelson and others like him usually begin with a noble goal, but try to achieve it in ways that simply will not work. The fact is, people will never become holy by submitting to a set of man-made rules. That's legalism, and it will never, ever work. Never!

Unfortunately, that doesn't stop people from trying. Legalists speak with tremendous force, authority, and enthusiasm on subjects about which the Bible maintains a discreet silence. That's basically what legalism is.

The Bible doesn't say anything about some things and very little about other things, and some folks simply aren't comfortable with that silence. They want to fill in the gaps. The problem comes when they begin to speak authoritatively about these gaps, in fact more authoritatively than even the Scripture itself. Then we are in danger of coming into the bondage of legalism.

It comes in two forms.

First, legalists will speak forcibly about what we must not do. That's what the legalists in Colossae were doing. They were telling the Colossians what they shouldn't eat and what they shouldn't drink. "You shall not eat this, this, and this," they said, "and you should not drink that, that, and that."

It wasn't that the Bible said anything to Christians on the subject; rather, it was what these people had concluded from their own thinking and teaching. They attempted to impose a structure on others that was biblically inappropriate.

Now, it's just possible that some of us have been exposed to this kind of thing. People have tried to lay upon us rules of behavior that have nothing to do with Scripture. Clearly the Bible sometimes says, "Thou shalt not." Clearly the Bible often says, "Thou shalt." I'm not talking about that sort of thing; I'm talking about people's saying, "You shall not eat this, you shall not drink this, you shall not go there, you shall not do that," even though the Bible says nothing about it. That is legalism.

Legalism also tells you what you *must* do. Apparently these teachers in the church at Colossae were insisting that people should observe religious festivals, New Moon celebrations, and the Sabbath day in a particular way. Notice that the religious festivals were annual, the New Moon celebrations were monthly, and the Sabbath was weekly. They were trying to get people into a rigid pattern of behavior on an annual, monthly, and weekly basis.

All of us are occasionally guilty of insisting that people do certain things, that they go certain places, that they perform certain rituals and adhere to certain practices. The Bible is silent about it, but we insist on these things.

Whenever we do that, we have lapsed into legalism.

People straining under legalism are in bondage. They become nervous and uptight, wondering if it's OK to do this and not that, if they should be here and not there, if they're correctly dotting their i's and crossing their t's.

Notice Paul's rebuttal of this approach. He says, "Don't let those kinds of people judge you."

Legalists tend not only to lay out for you a system of behavior explaining what to do and what not to do, but often go a step further and say, "If you don't do it this way, you're not spiritual." They judge you on the basis of their own principles of operation. Paul says there are two reasons you should oppose them.

First, these people don't understand that the things they are particularly concerned about are merely a shadow of what was fulfilled in Christ. They are confusing shadow with substance.

Second, while these people not infrequently are deeply into ritual, they're not especially interested in the deep, spiritual reality of which the ritual speaks.

If ever you find yourself coming into bondage to the systems of a legalistic-minded brother or sister, you need to take action. Don't let them put you in a box because you don't dot their i's and cross their t's. Paul says it's more than likely they are confusing shadow with substance and substituting ritual for reality. You don't need that.

What you do need is a fresh appreciation for the grace and freedom that is in Christ Jesus, a grace and freedom that lead to true godliness as the Holy Spirit brings the truth of God's Word to bear on your life.

Rules can't make you holy. Legalism can't produce righteousness. All it's good for is producing a certain smugness that eventually ends in disaster.

Just ask John Bockelson.

Beware!
That Umpire Is Out to Get You!

*Do not let anyone who delights in false humility
and the worship of angels disqualify you for the
prize. Such a person goes into great detail about
what he has seen, and his unspiritual mind puffs
him up with idle notions.*

t's a dangerous thing to think of yourself as an "expert."

Several years ago, three college students learned of a search for some unfinished sculptures that artist Amedeo Modigliani reportedly threw into a canal in Livorno, Italy. The students thought they'd have a little fun by carving their own masterworks out of a piece of sidewalk, dirtying them up with some grass, and heaving them into the canal.

When divers surfaced with the counterfeit sculptures a few days later, the response from art experts was immediate and thunderous.

"Authentic!" cried one.

"In these two scabrous stones there is the Annunciation, there is the Presence," shouted another.

"These stones have a soul," proclaimed a third.

The students were dumbfounded. They called the authorities and admitted their fraud, displaying photos for proof.

At least one expert refused to believe them. Wasn't he the art expert? Shouldn't he know the genuine article when he saw it? He thought so, and challenged the students to duplicate their efforts on national TV.

They did.

The expert turned red, the public chortled, and at least one of the students vowed that from then on he wouldn't let anyone tell him what to value as "good art."

Elitists, wherever they appear, deserve to be opposed. They deserved it in Livorno, and they deserved it in ancient Colossae.

In Colossae's case, the apostle played the role of the three students. Elitist teachers had infiltrated the Colossian church and were making all sorts of remarkable claims. They were super-saints in their own estimation. They thought they had the whole thing nailed down and insisted that others should toe their line.

Paul entered the picture and said, "Listen, friends, don't be misled by these 'experts.' Their claims are a fraud; they can't even recognize the real thing when they see it. Don't give in to them for a minute!"

You know, it's easy to be intimidated by elitists. They come in and speak with tremendous authority and charisma. They describe their own experiences in wonderful, compelling terms, and make us feel like worms.

"Oh, these super-spiritual giants," we moan. "Woe! I haven't even started. Woe is me!" We find ourselves in bondage to elitism.

Let's notice what was going on in Colossae. Paul says these teachers delighted in false humility. His phrase is a little difficult in the Greek, but he means something like this: It's good to be humble. The problem lies in a person's *delighting* in his humility. As soon as you start delighting in being humble, as soon as you become humble and get proud of it, you're not humble anymore. It is a false humility.

I can't explain it as well as a little piece of poetry:

Humility, the sweetest, loveliest flower that bloomed in Eden,
and the first that died,
has rarely blossomed since on mortal soil.

*It is so frail, so delicate a thing, it is gone if it but looks
upon itself,
and he who ventures to think it is his,
proves by that single thought he has it not.*

Some people in the spiritual realm are really into humility.
They're so impressed with how much of it they have that they
seek to impress it upon you. All such humility is phony, arrogant,
elitist, and leads only to bondage.

Paul mentions something else about these people of mock
humility—they worshiped angels. There are two ways to interpret
this.

One is that the gnostic teachers—those who saw spirit as
good and matter as bad, and who thought the only way to reach
God was through a series of intermediaries—were saying, "We
are so sinful and so humble about it that we can't approach God
on our own; we worship angels instead, trusting that they will
take our worship to God and present it to him. We do it like this
because we're too humble to come into God's presence ourselves."

This denies the Bible's clear teaching that there is but one
mediator between God and man, the man, Christ Jesus. Their
"humility" was false because while they pretended their sin
excluded them from the presence of the living God, they scorned
the new and living way to God that Christ provided. The fact is,
intermediaries aren't needed at all.

The second interpretation is that these people claimed to
worship in the same way that angels worship. This might tie in
with 1 Corinthians 13, where the apostle says, "If I speak with
the tongues of men or of angels and have not love . . ."

It may be that these people were claiming a special type
of worship where they spoke angel language and sang angel music,
moving thereby into God's presence in a way others could not.

We don't know which interpretation is right, but we can
identify Paul's major concern. He opposed an elitist approach to
worship. These people were claiming that the only way to approach
God was their way. Paul said, "You're wrong."

This should have been obvious the first time they opened
their mouths. An elitist teacher parted his lips and out came
boasts going "into great detail about what he has seen."

The expression translated "what he has seen" refers to special visions. Apparently these infiltrators of the church at Colossae claimed special visions and insights.

Now, when people claim to have a vision, there is nothing you can do about it. They either had it or they didn't. You can't say they did, you can't say they didn't. If a person has a vision and insists on telling you about it, the proper response is, "Really?" You don't need to go any further.

Be prepared, though, to get an earful.

"Listen," they'll say, "I have a vision, and this vision is for the church and this vision is for you, and you'd better listen up! If you don't do what this vision says, all kinds of calamity will come upon you!"

That is an entirely different matter, because now they are imposing upon you an elitist approach to Christianity. They and only they have this vision. There is no way of knowing if it is true, no way to check it out, no checks and balances. The only thing you can do is listen, hang loose, and wait to see if it happens. If it does, you can say they were either right or lucky. If it doesn't, you can say they're phony.

If this seems far removed from where you are today, let me report that in my mail I get an average of one vision and one prophecy per week. I got one just this week. I swear I did not commission it. This is what it says:

Dear Religious One,

On November 20, the following prophesy was received from the Lord for all who will be hearers:

The time and the hour and the day are at hand, even at our doorstep. The Spirit of the Lord says, repent, repent, repent, and return to the ways of the Lord God of all creation. For the iniquities of the heart of man have matured as with Cannanland and the woes of God are near at hand. Religion is not Christianity, there are many Jesuses, but only the faithful, humble, broken and repentative will ever know the true Jesus. This is the prophecy.

In this next year it will begin to happen, the fourth beast shall rise, this will fulfill the time prophesied

in Daniel 7 when the terrible beast shall rise to power
(which means politics) and crush so many when the
Pharisees, the ones who think themselves to be the
elect, who are the Baptists, begin to receive their power
for one hour with the dragon.

That's the vision. I know the writer is sincere and earnest,
because this thing was mailed out all over the country.

I want to assure you that people today are into this kind
of thing. They are into visions, they are into specific prophetic
ministries. They like to claim a special "in" with God which no
one can evaluate—it's just they and God. That's elitist.

What does Paul say about this? "Don't let these elitists
bring you into bondage," he writes. Literally, he says, "Don't let
them disqualify you." The Greek refers to an umpire who makes
a call against you.

These kinds of people come up to you and say, "Do you
delight in humility?"

"Oh, no," you say.

"Strike one!" they reply. "Do you worship angels?"

"Well, I'm not even sure what you mean."

"Strike two! Do you have visions?"

"Well, I dream."

"Yes, but do you have visions from God?"

"I don't think so."

"Strike three! You're out!"

That's the idea here. You didn't know baseball was in the
Bible? Well, you *would* if you could get into the original languages
like I can, and . . .

Oops! How easily we settle into elitism! Don't forget that
it's off limits to Christians. Don't let elitists disqualify you for the
prize. Let them have their visions.

You keep Jesus!

Beware!
That Diet May Hospitalize You!

Since you died with Christ to the basic principles
of this world, why, as though you still belonged
to it, do you submit to its rules: "Do not handle!
Do not taste! Do not touch!"? These are all
destined to perish with use, because they are
based on human commands and teachings. Such
regulations indeed have an appearance of
wisdom, with their self-imposed worship, their
false humility and their harsh treatment of the
body, but they lack any value in restraining
sensual indulgence.

If you had traveled to ancient Syria to see the famous Simeon Stylites, you would have met a pillar of the community in more ways than one.

Simeon was a fourth-century monk who directed a large group of disciples from atop a 60-foot pillar where he perched himself for more than thirty years. His meager needs were lifted to him in a basket.

Once, when some maggots fell from an open sore on Simeon's body, the monk asked that the creatures be returned to him, for "what God has given them to eat, I will not take away," he cried.

We wince at the thought, but it was nothing unusual for Simeon. He was an ascetic *par excellence*, dedicated to pursuing God by disregarding his body.

What's an ascetic, you ask? "Asceticism" comes from a Greek word which meant "to exercise" or "to go into training." Athletes got into it when they wanted to bring their bodies to peak performance.

As time went on, ascetics came to believe that conditioning their body would also enrich their mind. Later still the word "ascetic" came to describe someone who disciplined his body to get a deep spiritual experience. Enter Simeon Stylites.

Today the word is defined in the *Encyclopedia Britannica* as "The practice of the denial of physical or psychological desires in order to attain a spiritual ideal or goal."

Asceticism still has its followers in various segments of the Christian church. These people hope that by denying their physical or psychological desires, they might reach a specified spiritual goal. Fasting, celibacy, limitation of location, self-induced pain—they're all examples of asceticism.

We're not quite sure what brand of asceticism Paul was talking about in this passage, but we do know something about those who endorsed it.

First, they were dogmatic about it. In verse 20 Paul tells the Colossians not to submit to the ascetics' rules. The Greek word translated "submit to its rules" is nearly identical to our English word "dogmatize." These people were coming in to the church and dogmatically saying, "Do this with your body, do that with your body, touch this, don't touch that, handle this, don't handle that, don't taste that, don't taste this." They gave you a list of regulations as long as your arm about how to handle your body in order to stimulate a spiritual experience.

The apostle identifies their dogmatism, then refutes it. He says, in effect, "Friends, why on earth are you submitting to this approach? Why are you letting these ascetics bring you into bondage? These people are concerned about mere physical things, which cease to exist the moment you use them."

What Paul means is this: Suppose you have a beautiful strawberry shortcake in front of you. You extend your hand, pick up your fork, open your mouth, and very soon strawberry shortcake ceases to exist. It has perished with the using. So why eat it?

That's an approach to dieting you will not have thought of before. It's basically what the apostle is saying, though; the moment you use the food, it ceases to exist as food. So what's the big deal about it?

Ascetics will try to get you into all kinds of body control and mind control and diet control in an effort to achieve a spiritual high. But it won't work.

Why not? It's very simple.

A fleshly cure cannot remedy a spiritual disease. Tinkering with the body can't fix a malfunction of the soul. A sick man's heart won't get better by clipping his toenails.

When ascetics try to stimulate heavenly experiences by tapping earthly methods, their approach is all wrong. The reason it won't work goes to the heart of Christ's purpose in coming to earth in the first place.

Sinful man can never reach God through his own efforts. No matter how earnest the effort, no matter how agonizing the labor, no matter how severe the method, sinful man can never bridge the chasm between himself and a holy God. It was to bridge that chasm that Christ came to earth and died on a cross. Fleshly effort, either before or after a person's conversion, chalks up no points with God.

Listen—do you really think God would put his Son through the humiliation and agony of the cross if all that was needed for us to get right with God and have good spiritual experiences was a little dieting here and a little skin whacking there?

Sin is a horrible, deadly affliction whose cure demands the very wisdom and power of God Almighty. Human cunning and strength will never do. Ascetic practices are doomed to failure, Paul says, "because they are based on human commands and teachings."

Nevertheless, people still try them. The remarkable thing is that none of these approaches actually discourages sins of the flesh. In fact, they "lack any value in restraining sensual indulgence," according to Paul.

It's a well-cataloged fact that the deeper ascetics get into their practices, the more appalled they become at the increasing sinfulness of their own hearts. Asceticism simply can't deliver the goods.

It can put on an impressive show, however, and that's no doubt why so many continue to try it. "Such regulations," Paul writes, "indeed have an appearance of wisdom, with their self-imposed worship, their false humility and their harsh treatment of the body."

Asceticism may not work, but it looks good. In an image-conscious culture, appearance counts for a lot.

For years, a stately oak tree stood guard over a neighborhood. Families came and went, but the tree remained. It was old and big and thick and gnarled, the pride of the block it overshadowed. Passers-by admired the ancient tree for its beauty and strength.

Then one night a storm crashed into town. Nothing major—just a typical storm for that time of year.

Dawn came, and with it a shock. As neighbors gazed out their windows, everywhere they saw large clumps of twisted oak branches strewn about the ground, far more branches than such a storm should have torn loose. The big, thick, majestic oak tree looked bare.

A hasty investigation showed that while the old tree wore a cloak of strength and power, it was thoroughly rotten inside. It looked good, but was dying. Had it toppled over—as it could have at the slightest breeze—its dead hulk would have crushed anyone in its way.

That's the problem with looking good when there's nothing but rottenness inside. People can be greatly impressed with a terrific appearance . . . and never know that they're close to being flattened.

Don't be deceived by the lure of the ascetics, Paul says. They may look good and sound good, but inside is nothing but decay. If you want true spiritual experience, stick with Christ. If your heart is cold and stony and malfunctioning, you don't need your toenails clipped. You need a new heart.

Dr. Jesus is the only one who can give it to you.

Beware!
That Balance Beam Is Tilted!

Grace be with you.

Many years ago Jill and I were talking with some English collegians who had returned home after their first year at university. We spent a whole wonderful afternoon answering their questions.

At the end of our time together, one of the students said, "Stuart, every single answer you have given has included 'balance.' A lot of it sounds like compromise to me. Can you explain the difference between balance and compromise?"

"That's the easiest question of the afternoon," I replied. "If you do it, it's compromise. If I do it, it's balance."

Balance. If there's one thing in the spiritual life we must maintain, it's balance. God's truth is often found in tension, and we must take care never to emphasize one aspect of truth over another. Let me give an example.

The Bible clearly teaches the sovereignty of God. It also clearly teaches the free will of man. That makes for some tension.

Some don't want to handle the tension, and so become either resolute free-will Arminians or staunch sovereignty-of-God

Calvinists. The two groups separated centuries ago and have been shooting at each other ever since.

When people don't want to balance the tension, the easiest thing in the world is to opt for one side and take it to an unintended extreme . . . and create a breeding ground for heresy.

Paul always tried to caution against an extremism that disallows balancing aspects of truth. He taught the necessity of holding in tension the truths of Scripture so that no truth is pushed to a heretical end.

When he says legalism is out, he doesn't mean that anything goes. When he says elitism is out, he doesn't mean you should strive for mediocrity. When he says asceticism is out, he doesn't mean we should become ill-disciplined slobs.

In all these things there must be balance.

It is in this area we need to study and to pray and to mature and to grow. If we don't, then somebody, somewhere, will bring us into bondage.

"Oh, I see what you mean, Stuart," you say. "You're saying that balance is the key. That helps a great deal—thank you very much."

Whoa, hold on! You may have been listening too much to my lectures to my college friends. Balance, as important as it is, is not the key thought in Paul's message.

The central idea can be summed up in one word: freedom.

Paul writes to tell us that we are not to allow ourselves to be brought into bondage to anything, anywhere, anymore. He sums it up best in Galatians 5:1: "It is for freedom that Christ has set us free. Stand firm, then, and do not let yourselves be burdened again by a yoke of slavery." We are free!

"Free to be what?" you say.

"Free to be myself!" replies society.

"No, no!" says the Bible. "You're free to be *Christ's*. Therefore, don't let anyone bring you into any kind of bondage that would deny you the freedom to be exclusively his."

Let's get that clear! You are free to be Christ's, and to be his alone. This is true freedom—a freedom so invigorating, so full and lively and bracing and dynamic, that it's impossible to fully describe. You have to experience it. Perhaps an illustration would help.

Some of the best high school basketball in the nation is played in the state of Illinois. When early spring rolls around and winter sneaks away, you can be sure that basketball junkies will plop themselves in front of the tube to watch the annual state tournament. A few of these teams look as good as those suiting up for small colleges.

Every year after the champions have been crowned, local television stations interview the winning players. One year a fabulously talented team from the Chicago area won the title. A reporter asked the team's starting center how he felt about winning. I'm sure the interviewer thought he was about to hear some familiar lines: "Oh, I feel great! This is the best ever! We worked hard for it," that sort of thing.

Was he disappointed. All the kid did was talk about cows.

That's right, cows. The lad had never seen any, and some friends had promised him a trip to a Wisconsin farm if his team won. It did, and shortly he'd be nuzzling the heifers. He had never touched a cow, never heard a cow moo, and certainly had never milked one. His experience was cowless.

The interview, as I recall, went something like this:

"So, how does it feel to be champion?"

"Good. I hope I get to see one of them white and brown ones. The ones with the big spots."

"Ah, yes. Well, did you expect the game to be easy?"

"Yah. Have you ever seen whole crowds of 'em, all sittin' around like they ain't got nothin' to do? Man!"

"Let's talk about the game, son. How did you prepare for this big game?"

"I never seen any. I only seen 'em in books. Do you think they'd let me touch one?"

"Yes, well, about the game . . ."

"I mean, whadda they do all day? Do they bite? Do they really eat *grass*? Do they got names? And what's cud? Can ya eat it?"

301

The interview never did get around to hoops. Final score: Basketball 0, Bossy 4.

You know, there's an enormous difference between talking about something wonderful and experiencing that wonderful thing for yourself. We could talk all day about the joys of being united to Christ or about the freedom you'll find in him, but until you make the trip yourself it will only be a report.

If a young man from Chicago could get so thrilled about seeing his first cow, I guarantee you that walking with the one who made every cow on a thousand hills will far surpass anything you've ever known.

Don't settle for reports! Don't get waylaid by counterfeits! Experience Christ for yourself!

You were made for a glorious relationship with King Jesus, and only when you are rooted and growing and established in him will you truly enjoy all that life has to offer. When Paul ends his letters, "Grace be with you," that's what he's talking about.

Do you want fulfillment? Then stick with Jesus!

Do you want contentment? Then stick with Jesus!

Do you want spiritual health? Then stick with Jesus!

It's the only way to develop a spiritual stamina that lasts!

Working Out

1. The best way to avoid disastrous error is to stay close to Christ. That is why every time Paul warns his Christian friends about deceivers who would try to bring them into bondage, he points back to Christ.

In Colossians 2:8, the apostle directs his friends' attention to Christ. They don't need to follow empty tradition or false philosophy; everything they need is found in Christ.

In Colossians 2:16-17, Paul warns the church to reject any teaching that would put them in bondage to rules of eating or drinking or mandatory rituals. He says the only thing these rules were meant to do is to foreshadow Christ; they certainly don't replace him. Everything they dimly pictured is available in full measure in Christ.

In Colossians 2:18-19, Paul warns the church against elitism. Elitists have forgotten that Christ is the one who holds everything together and who directs the Christian body. If the Colossians wanted to grow in their walk with God, they needed to be rightly connected to the Head, Jesus Christ.

In Colossians 2:20-23, Paul begins his repudiation of asceticism by reminding his readers that they had already died with Christ. Fleshly approaches to the spiritual life are purely manmade and can never bring men and women into a right relationship with God. Jesus provides the only possible way into the Father's presence.

A. If the best way to protect yourself from spiritual danger is to remind yourself of who Christ is and what he has done for you, what plan do you have to see that your mind will constantly be fixed on Christ? Do you have a regular schedule for reading the Gospels? Do you have friends with whom you talk about Jesus? Do you have regular times of conversation with Christ in prayer? Do you happily mention him to those who don't know him? Try to develop a plan of your own, share your plan with someone else, and ask him or her to hold you accountable to it.

B. Pick one of Paul's shorter letters and count the number of times he mentions "Jesus" or "Christ" or "the Lord." Notice the language he uses to describe Christ—is it joyful? Emotional? Passionate? Does this suggest anything about building a strong faith?

Second Wind

1. Matthew 24:3-14
   As the time gets closer for Jesus to return, how will deceivers try to turn people away from God?

2. Acts 20:25-32
   Are the dangers that confront Christians limited to deceivers who come into the church from the outside?

3. Galatians 1:6-9
   How important is it to keep straight the teaching of the gospel? Should we be willing to change the story if a mighty angel would tell us to?

4. Philippians 3:1-11
   Why does Paul repeat himself in this passage? Would we do well to imitate his method?

5. 1 Timothy 4:1-5
   What universal principle given here helps to identify false teachers?